T0358053

YOU WON'T F*CK IT UP

**BUYING PROPERTY IS EASIER
THAN YOU THINK**

You
Won't
F*ck
It Up

DOMENIC NESCI

MAJOR
STREET

I would like to dedicate this book to my beautiful fiancée Charlotte and my son Leonardo. Thank you Charlotte for your patience and support. I chose to write this book at a very busy time in our lives but you were always there to cheer me on and create the space for me to work. Leonardo, this first year of your life has been a joy and source of motivation for me to build you a bright future. I love you both very much.

MAJOR STREET

First published in 2023 by Major Street Publishing Pty Ltd
info@majorstreet.com.au | +61 421 707 983 | majorstreet.com.au

© Domenic Nesci 2023
The moral rights of the author have been asserted.

A catalogue record for this book is available from the National Library of Australia

Printed book ISBN: 978-1-922611-63-5
Ebook ISBN: 978-1-922611-64-2

All rights reserved. Except as permitted under *The Australian Copyright Act 1968* (for example, a fair dealing for the purposes of study, research, criticism or review), no part of this book may be reproduced, stored in a retrieval system, communicated or transmitted in any form or by any means without prior written permission. All inquiries should be made to the publisher.

Cover design by Typography Studio
Internal design by Production Works
Printed in Australia by IVE, an accredited ISO 9001 Quality Management and ISO 14001 Environmental Management Printer.

10 9 8 7 6 5 4 3 2 1

Disclaimer: The material in this publication is in the nature of general comment only, and neither purports nor intends to be advice. Readers should not act on the basis of any matter in this publication without considering (and if appropriate taking) professional advice with due regard to their own particular circumstances. The author and publisher expressly disclaim all and any liability to any person, whether a purchaser of this publication or not, in respect of anything and the consequences of anything done or omitted to be done by any such person in reliance, whether whole or partial, upon the whole or any part of the contents of this publication.

Contents

Preface

Buying property is easier than you think. Whether you are buying your own home or an investment property, there are only so many variables for you to consider, and most of the profit comes from simply picking something good and then having the patience to wait for it to grow.

My old boss was a grey-haired veteran financial planner who had been in the business all his life. When I first started there, he would often say to me, 'Investing in property is easy, you just need to not f*ck it up'. What he meant by this was to keep it simple. Most people he saw who overcomplicated things by pushing too hard to outperform the market were met with frustration, financial losses and many hard-earned lessons. This is a truth that I have experienced personally and seen with many investors.

In *You Won't F*ck It Up* I am going to pass on many of these hard-earned lessons and give you a bunch of easy-to-understand information about how to invest in property. I am going to show you how to avoid f*cking it up.

Before we kick it all off, I want to tell you a little bit about myself. After all, anyone can call themselves an expert in real estate, and many do. This is, in fact, one of the problems in our industry, which leads to a lot of misinformation and a lack of trust. So, here's a quick overview of me and my journey to date.

I fell in love with real estate at a very young age. I can remember driving around with my divorced mother window-shopping and dreaming of being able to buy different houses. She would tell me about how much the houses cost years earlier and we would estimate how much they had grown in value. The people who had bought these houses had made fortunes and seemed to us to be very rich.

We did not have a lot of money, and this put constant pressure on our daily lives. Seeing these homes that provided wealth and security inspired me to strive for this same security for my family.

I started working at age 15 and read every book that I could get my hands on about investing and real estate. Seven years later I was working as a financial planner and had bought my first property.

I am now 35 and have lived around the world, advised on over a billion dollars' worth of real estate and have a multimillion-dollar property portfolio that has brought my family the security that I had always dreamed of. My passion for property and drive to help others led me to create a property investment business called Wealthi.

Wealthi's purpose is to make property investment easy. We have educated thousands of people about real estate investment and helped hundreds of clients start and build real estate portfolios that have brought their households the same security I desired as a child.

The goal of this book is to help you buy property and not f*ck it up. I want to help you make smart decisions about the real estate you buy and potentially build a portfolio that will create wealth and set you free financially. This is an easy-to-understand guide that you can refer to as you venture through your own property investment journey.

This book dives into key themes that you should be mindful of when buying real estate and breaks them down into what you need to know, why it is important and how you can find this information. It will give you the tools and confidence to become a successful real estate investor. And, don't worry, you won't f*ck it up!

PART I

The Big Picture

When you are searching for property and first land on a property site such as realestate.com.au or domain.com.au, you are asked to type in the suburb, postcode or state. So, as a purchaser, the first important consideration is, *Where am I going to buy?* This is the big question that all real estate buyers ask themselves, and big questions require big thinking.

To answer this question, you need to zoom out and look carefully at the big picture. This is what the first part of this book covers.

There are five key factors that make up the big picture:

1. *Outlook:* What will this area look like in 3, 5 or 10 years?
2. *Population:* Are there more people coming into the area than moving away?
3. *Infrastructure:* Are there plans for new roads, schools and hospitals to be built in this area?
4. *Employment:* Can residents find work locally, or will they need to commute?
5. *Supply:* Are there lots of properties on the market, do they change hands often and are there plans to build more homes in the future?

When buying real estate, you want to look as far into the future as you can, since generally, the longer you hold the asset, the better your returns will be over time. Being aware of what is happening here and now is great to secure the deal that you want in order to make short-term gains, but real growth comes from compounding returns, which can provide seismic shifts over periods of 5, 10 and 20 years.

This look into the future is the outlook, which is covered in chapter 1. The next three considerations – population, infrastructure and employment – contribute to the outlook for the location where you are thinking of buying. They will determine the potential future demand for property in this area. The final consideration, supply, will help you work out how easy or hard it will be for you to enter this market.

Chapter 1

Outlook

To determine the economic and real estate market outlook, you first need to know what is happening in the market now. Is it a buyers' or sellers' market at the moment, and is this likely to change in the near future?

In a buyers' market, there are not many buyers out there. If a property is on the market in these conditions, it means the vendor (the seller) needs to sell. This makes negotiating with the vendors easier. You have the power. The conditions are in your favour. Perhaps you can buy the property for a discount or negotiate more favourable terms.

In a sellers' market, negotiating is very hard because there are many other buyers behind you also trying to purchase the property. Maybe they are willing to pay more, and so they are pushing up the value. The power in this situation rests with the seller.

The easiest way to visualise the difference is to imagine an auction: are you the only person who makes a bid, or is there a bunch of other buyers who keep bidding against you?

In a buyers' market you can take your time and drag your feet with the vendor, but in a sellers' market you typically need to be decisive and make your best offer to get that property off the market as soon as possible.

There are three things that contribute to current and future market conditions, which all influence whether you are facing a buyers' or sellers' market:

1. finance
2. government policy
3. sentiment.

Understand these three things and you'll be better equipped to understand the market outlook and adopt the best strategies to buy in these conditions.

Finance

There's an old saying in the property world: 'Money is not made by timing the market, but rather by time in the market'. This is broadly true, and it's meant to educate two groups of new investors: the first who might overthink their first purchase and the second who might try to become developer 'flippers' too soon.

Lots of would-be investors fall victim to overthinking things. They spend years saving their deposit waiting for the market to fall rather than taking that leap of faith and using the market to their advantage. Their view is this: 'Just as my parents did, once I have saved a 20 per cent deposit, I'm going to wait for the property market to fall and I'll find the perfect home that I can fall in love with'. The problem is that times have changed. The average Australian first homebuyer is now in their 30s and it takes them up to 11.4 years to save a 20 per cent deposit (see figure 1)!

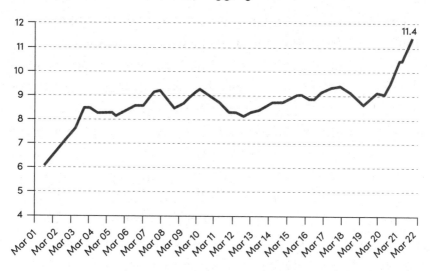

Figure 1: Years required to save a 20 per cent deposit – national aggregates

SOURCE: ANU, ANZ CORELOGIC HOUSING AFFORDABILITY REPORT 2022

In that time, this would-be homeowner could have bought an investment property – or a much more affordable home that was not perfect – at the four-year mark and let this property grow for seven years, which is about a full market cycle. If they had invested $75,000 (a 10 per cent deposit plus stamp duty and costs) into a $500,000 property and it grew by an average of 7 per cent, it would be worth about $984,000, making them a profit of $484,000. To achieve this same return they would have to save $50,000 per year in after-tax dollars. Needless to say, the average Australian cannot save this much.

The second group, the would-be developers, is focused on trying to time the market in a different way. They speculate on timing by waiting for a 'dip' in prices to buy, then selling or flipping out of property when they think they've reached the top of a cycle. More money has been lost overthinking and speculating than doing the simple thing, which is to pick a good property, buy it when you can afford it, then *hold*!

The simple truth here is that it pays to understand what is happening in the market because 'what' will help you more than 'when'. When buying real estate, you need to know when to move fast and slow. Understanding market conditions will help you do this.

In March 2020 COVID-19 really started to have an impact around the world and, over the course of that year, we saw countries go into different degrees of lockdown, people start working from home and governments discuss different types of stimulus models. This was a great time to buy property. There was a lot of uncertainty and people were very nervous about what was going to happen next; as a property investor, I could see opportunities all over the market.

At that time, my business partner Peter and I were recording the Wealthi podcast and we were on air, talking like madmen, telling people to buy property. We could see the following developments that were certain to stimulate the market after COVID-19:

- Governments around the world were printing *huge* sums of money to inject into the economy.
- The Australian government had created some very big first-homebuyer incentives along with builder bonuses and, at the state level, some governments were offering stamp duty concessions.
- The interest rate was at an all-time low and looking to go lower.

When the media was showing us shops and businesses closing and people staying at home, we saw something different. We saw that there was going to be a pile of money coming into the economy through government grants and other stimuli, and on top of this people were saving their money because they couldn't go out and spend it. We predicted that there was going to be a wave of first homebuyers looking to get out of their smaller rental properties and into their own homes as soon as they could.

This is exactly what happened. We saw an owner-occupier and first-homebuyer-led property market recovery. According to the CoreLogic Daily Home Value Index, between April 2020 and February 2022 housing prices in Australia jumped by 24.6 per cent. The total value of residential real estate soared from $7.2 trillion at the start of the pandemic to $9.8 trillion. The median dwelling value increased by $173,805, from $554,229 to $728,034.

Peter and I did not have a crystal ball, but we did know that people's motivations are pretty clear and people respond in predictable ways. We knew that, when people are offered free or really cheap money, they tend to spend it.

Case study: buying my holiday house in Nelson Bay

Here's how this situation affected my buying decisions personally. My fiancée Charlotte and I (and our dog, Apollo) were rentvesting in a little two-bedroom apartment in the Sydney beachside suburb of Coogee. We had bought an investment property in the western suburbs of Sydney at the end of 2019 and we needed time to build our finances back up before we could buy again. This was frustrating because we could see that it was a great time to buy, but we simply were not ready yet.

By the end of 2020, the property market started to show some early signs of recovery but, as Australia went in and out of different lockdowns, offices and the CBDs were still largely shut down. Peter and I were working remotely, like most other Australians, and we noticed that there was a shift in the air. Perhaps, after COVID-19, people would like things to stay this way – they might still prefer to work from home, and not necessarily in the major cities.

It was near the end of 2020 that we began to talk more about tree changes and sea changes on the podcast. As investors we believed that, since money was so cheap and people could effectively work from home, home could now be one, two, three or even four hours from the office. We predicted that there would be a shift away from inner-city, high-density living to more affordable, bigger homes offering a better lifestyle away from CBDs. People were feeling cooped up at home and wanted space and, since they did not need to commute to work in the cities anymore, why not move their families further away?

After the big wave of first-homebuyer and builder-bonus stimulus packages, owner-occupiers started to upgrade their homes, moving to something bigger, often outside the major cities. Shortly after, we saw the property market pick up and property prices rocket, with houses in regional centres leading the growth.

Charlotte and I had begun our property hunt for a little retreat three hours outside of Sydney. We had spent three months or so making short trips up and down the coast looking for a property that met our criteria and budget, while at the same time we were organising our finances. This was a slow process of research and discovery.

It was both a fun and frustrating experience: fun hunting for homes, seeing new areas and dreaming of a new life in these properties, but very frustrating watching these properties sell and the prices move further out of our reach week after week. However, this process was extremely valuable. With every market we visited, we learnt more about what we wanted and, more importantly, didn't want. With each property, we learnt what we were prepared to pay and how much time we were happy to invest.

When we finally got our financial approval, we knew exactly what we wanted and how much we were prepared to pay. This is when we moved fast.

We had narrowed down our search to the Port Stephens area. We wanted the home to be within walking distance of the beaches and town. We didn't want to spend more than $700,000 and were happy to buy something that needed a lot of work. The dream for us was to find a property with a view but we knew this was unlikely due to the budget.

When you are hunting for a property, you become very familiar with the market, and you should know just about every property that becomes available for sale. At this point in time, as we had been researching this area for some time, I did.

So, when a property in Nelson Bay (in the Port Stephens area) came onto the market one Friday that met all our requirements, plus it had a view, I was immediately interested. The advertised price was $580,000 to $640,000 and it was a sellers' market. On the Monday, I called the agent and offered $650,000 for them to send me a contract of sale and take the property off the market. As we had done our research, secured our finance and were able to move fast, we got the contract and bought the property.

During COVID-19 some regional centres grew by more than 40 per cent. With a bit of good luck and a lot of hard work, we made a significant amount of equity in the Nelson Bay property very quickly. Soon after buying the property, there was another wave of COVID-19, and Charlotte told me that she was pregnant with our first baby. So, we decided to spend our lockdown in Nelson Bay and renovate the house. After spending 12 months and about $70,000 on the renovations, we had the property valued at just over $1 million.

We learnt a few lessons from this experience:

- Having a strong understanding of what is happening in the market gives you, the buyer, power.
- Knowing how people behave during different financial and economic cycles, along with how they will respond to government policy, helps you predict what is likely to happen next. You'll be able to capitalise on opportunities that may be staring you in the face.

- In different economic conditions it pays to know when you need to act fast or slow. At the peak of COVID-19 it was a buyers' market. If you kept a level head, you could afford to slow down a negotiation and push a vendor to get the best deal. When the market is starting to run and favour sellers, as a buyer you no longer have this luxury of pushing vendors to the limit. You need to act fast to close the deal. You definitely don't want to end up at an auction and get caught in the emotional maelstrom that drives prices to new heights.

*

As I mentioned at the beginning of this part, the first question property buyers ask themselves is usually *Where am I going to buy?* but they can only answer this when they know the answer to the question *How much can I afford?* The more money people can borrow, the more they are likely to spend.

Access to credit tells investors how much they can afford to spend on a property. The easier and cheaper it is to get a loan, the more people you will see buying property. This is a great indicator of activity and how much demand you can expect to see in the market. When you have many new people entering the market, this represents an increase in demand and, provided supply stays the same or decreases, it is likely that property prices will go up. Conversely, the more difficult it is to get money, the less activity there will be in the market.

Access to finance is a huge lever that impacts demand.

So, how can you establish whether finance is easy to obtain? Here are a few questions to ask to find out:

- Is it easier or harder to borrow money from the banks?
- Are loans getting more expensive or cheaper with interest rates going up or down?

- What are the current banking policies?
- Which lenders are giving out the loans (tier one and/or tier two lenders)? What type of loans are they offering – owner-occupiers' principal-and-interest loans or investors' interest-only loans? What loan-to-value ratios (LVRs) are they accepting?

Let's go over some of the fundamentals of finance, the jargon and terminology you'll need to get your head around so you can have a more productive conversation with brokers and banks. This section also contains a few tips to consider when getting a loan and what to avoid so you have the best chance of securing a loan with favourable terms.

Lenders

To begin with, let's talk about the different banks, credit unions and other nonbank institutions that you can apply to get money from. They are all very different and become more or less relevant depending on how you earn a living, your credit history, the type of loan you want and how much you are applying for.

One thing I want to tell you before you read further is that, when you are applying for a loan, the interest rate is not the most important thing. The most important thing is getting a loan on time and with favourable terms. You certainly want to get the best rate you can, but I have seen many people chase a rate only to learn they will not be able to get it. They have had to rewrite their loan many times, causing stress, pushing deadlines and missing opportunities.

In Australia there are two tiers of lenders. Tier one is the traditional banks: the 'Big 4' of Westpac, Commonwealth Bank of Australia (CBA), ANZ Bank and National Australia Bank (NAB), as well as smaller regional banks such as the Bank of Melbourne or the Bank of Queensland. These banks typically offer the lowest rates, good banking facilities and different types of loan structures. The major banks have subtly different credit policies and appetites for different types of loans and properties, along with service-level agreements (SLAs; the amount of time they take to assess your loan application).

Although tier one lenders are generally the cheapest, they are harder to get loans from and, depending on what's happening in the market, can be the slowest to respond to your application. They are inflexible and generally harder to deal with if you have complicated finances, non-standard income or too much debt relative to your income.

They are good to use if you have a strong income, good savings and work in one of their favoured professions. In fact, some banks will give you a discount or better loan terms if you work in the medical field, or as a lawyer or chartered accountant.

Tier two lenders are nonbank entities such as credit unions or building societies. Examples include Pepper Money, RAMS, La Trobe Financial and Newcastle Permanent Building Society. Many of these institutions get their funds from the big banks. Because tier two lenders are nonbank entities, they are exempt from some of the more rigorous Australian Prudential Regulation Authority (APRA) rules imposed on banks.

If you have non-traditional income (anything other than PAYG), a new business, a small deposit, too much debt relative to your income, tight servicing or a need for fast approval, these institutions can be your best friends. I have used these businesses on many occasions; they are great for getting you out of tight situations and giving you money when you really want to get your loan.

Since these lenders have looser policies, the loans they write are typically seen as higher risk and are therefore priced appropriately. When applying for a loan, the more difficult and non-standard your application, the higher the interest rate will be. So, when things are tight, these lenders will likely give you a loan but will charge you more. However, as your circumstances improve over time, you can always refinance with one of the banks and get more favourable terms.

Loan structures and terminology

When you apply for a loan, there are a lot of subtle nuances that can have a huge impact on you and your life. Understanding these nuances is very important because they can either make your life easier or much more stressful. At first it may all seem too difficult to understand but, after a little reading and seeing the effects of these nuances in practice, it will all make sense. The great news is that you do not need to understand everything back to front – you just need to understand enough to be able to ask your bank or broker for what you want.

First, let's look at how you repay your loan. The 'principal' is the debt and the 'interest' is the fee you pay to the bank for giving you the loan. Banks want you to have a principal-and-interest (P&I) loan because it means you will be paying back your loan over time. These loans are normally set over a 30-year term (the amount of time to pay back the loan), but you can pay the loan back faster. When applying for this type of loan, banks will give you lower interest rates than for an interest-only (IO) loan because it is less risky. You can pay off a P&I loan as fast as you like in lump sums. This is the best loan structure for your own home.

An example of the way you pay off your debt is shown in figure 2 and table 1, overleaf.

Notice that, early on, you are mostly paying off the interest owed to the bank; over time, the proportion of your repayments that goes towards interest reduces and you pay off more of your principal.

One important little hack to remember here is that your interest is charged daily, so increasing the frequency of your repayments means you pay off your loan faster. This can have a big impact on your loan term, since paying down the loan faster means you get charged less interest on your loan.

Figure 2: P&I loan repayments

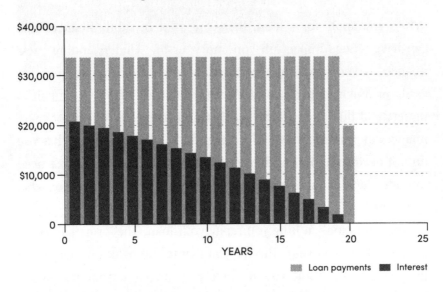

Table 1: Paying off a P&I loan

Year	Home value	Interest	Loan repayment	Loan balance	Home equity
0	$600,000			$420,000	$180,000
1	$624,000	$20,706	$33,672	$407,333	$216,967
2	$648,960	$20,042	$33,672	$393,403	$255,557
3	$674,918	$19,345	$33,672	$379,075	$295,843
4	$701,915	$18,612	$33,672	$364,015	$337,901
5	$729,992	$17,841	$33,672	$348,183	$381,808
6	$759,191	$17,031	$33,672	$331,542	$427,649
7	$789,559	$16,180	$33,672	$314,050	$475,509
8	$821,141	$15,285	$33,672	$295,662	$525,479
9	$853,987	$14,344	$33,672	$276,334	$577,653
10	$888,147	$13,355	$33,672	$256,017	$632,130
11	$923,672	$12,316	$33,672	$234,660	$689,012

Year	Home value	Interest	Loan repayment	Loan balance	Home equity
12	$960,619	$11,223	$33,672	$212,211	$748,408
13	$999,044	$10,075	$33,672	$188,613	$810,431
14	$1.039m	$8867	$33,672	$163,808	$875,197
15	$1.081m	$7598	$33,672	$137,734	$942,832
16	$1.124m	$6264	$33,672	$110,326	$1.013m
17	$1.169m	$4862	$33,672	$81,516	$1.087m
18	$1.215m	$3388	$33,672	$51,231	$1.164m
19	$1.264m	$1839	$33,672	$19,398	$1.245m
20	$1.315m	$326	$19,723	$0	$1.315m
21	$1.367m	$0	$0	$0	$1.367m
22	$1.422m	$0	$0	$0	$1.422m
23	$1.479m	$0	$0	$0	$1.479m
24	$1.538m	$0	$0	$0	$1.538m
25	$1.6m	$0	$0	$0	$1.6m

The alternative to a P&I loan is an IO loan, whereby you pay interest only as a way of servicing the loan and do not pay down any of the loan. The first thought many new property owners have is, *Why would I want a loan that I do not pay down?* The simple answer is that you do it for cash flow.

IO loans are primarily used by investors. Servicing only the interest allows the investor to keep more money in the bank to reinvest while also keeping their deductible debt high. Later in the book I briefly touch on taxes but, to cut a long story short, you can put the interest paid on the investment on your tax return as an expense to reduce your taxable income, thereby reducing the amount of tax you need to pay.

When setting up your loan, you can typically ask the lender to make the interest-only period between one and five years, and some banks will go up to ten years. However, this loan structure is seen as riskier for the bank because, for a period of time, you are not paying back the loan. To compensate for this additional risk, banks will increase the amount of interest you need to pay them and assess your ability to pay the loan at a higher servicing because, after you complete your interest-only period, they need to see that you can repay the principal in the time left on the loan.

Regardless of whether you choose a P&I or IO loan, you need to consider the rate at which you pay back the interest on the loan. This can be either variable or fixed. With a variable loan, the interest rate changes with the market's cash rate. The Reserve Bank of Australia (RBA) determines Australia's cash rate, and the banks typically add 2 to 3 per cent to this rate when charging customers. Having a variable rate gives you flexibility to refinance your loan along with the rises and falls of the market.

On the other hand, a fixed rate will not change for a nominated period of time. Fixed rates are a great way to ensure predictability with your loan repayments since you know exactly what they will be from month to month. During a time of rising interest rates, lenders will usually set fixed rates higher than the market, and when rates are falling they will apply discounts.

Keeping track of the fixed rates lenders are offering gives you an idea of how they see the economy and whether or not they think the rates will rise or fall. Banks will generally offer a fixed-rate period of between one and five years but, the longer this period is, the more difficult the servicing will be. While the rate of your loan is fixed, you are limited in how much of it you can pay off, and you usually will not be able to refinance your property without paying some kind of break fee.

To balance out your loan, you can opt to have a portion of your rate fixed and the rest variable.

Banking policy

This may seem boring but understanding some of the fundamentals of banking policy will give you enough firepower to work effectively with brokers and banks.

Each institution has their own appetite for different types of loans. Their policies are extremely varied, but they all come back to how they determine the risk as a lender. Here are a few key examples of the factors that can vary:

- *Debt-to-income (DTI) ratio:* The DTI ratio is a quick way to determine how much debt you can service on your income. This is generally around 1:6 or 1:7; so, if you are earning $100,000 per year then you can get a loan of about $600,000 to $700,000. Some of the nonbank lenders will go up to 1:9 or may not use this ratio at all. Some banks will deny your loan outright on the basis of a too-high DTI ratio.

- *Loan-to-value ratio (LVR):* The lower your LVR, the less risky the loan is, since there is more equity available to weather market shocks, and if you need to sell the property the bank will be repaid. It is generally accepted that an LVR of 80 per cent (80 per cent loan and 20 per cent cash and equity) is comfortable for banks. There are fewer and lower fees and no lenders mortgage insurance (LMI), and it is easier to refinance later. As a property owner, getting to this deposit threshold is the hardest bit, so a higher LVR makes it much easier to buy a property. This percentage has changed over the years: banks once accepted 100 per cent loans, but some have now retracted all the way to 70 per cent loans.

- *Transparency and disclosures:* Loans can be described as either 'low doc' (low or limited documentation) or 'full doc' (full documentation). Which is available depends on the institution and the loan structure. The more transparent you need to be, the harder you are going to be assessed, but the cheaper your rate will be. The opposite is also true: the less documentation you need to provide, the more relaxed the lender will be in their assessment of your finances, but they will charge you a higher rate since the loan is riskier for them.

- *Income:* Lenders all have different ways of determining your income and how it is received. Someone who runs their own business is considered 'self-employed' and therefore assessed differently to someone who is 'employed'. If you are 'employed', you will be assessed as riskier or more stable depending on your type of employment (casual, part-time, maternity leave, full-time, contractor, foreign income and so on). Lenders also assess rental income differently: some will take into account 100 per cent of your rental income while others will only take 80 per cent into account, or maybe even less.

- *Loan types and properties:* Each lender has different criteria for the types of properties they are happy to lend against and the loans they will write. For instance, some lenders will be happy to deal with house-and-land construction facilities, self-managed super funds and commercial loans, while others will not touch these types of structures. Some banks will not lend in certain areas at certain times due to density (they already have a bunch of properties in the location) or risk of overexposure (they determine the area to be too risky for them).

The lenders set their lending policies and terms according to many variables, but a key thing to note is that these policies and terms are not set in stone: they are rewritten depending on market conditions and provide a good indication of how the market is changing or is likely to change. These institutions hire very clever risk analysts and economists to determine what the property market is likely to do next and, if you pay attention, they'll give you some handy tips – not to mention opportunities to make money with your own lending facilities.

Here's an example of how I was able to take advantage of lending policy changes to release $320,000 from a loan, which allowed me to reinvest and make $26,400 in additional passive income annually. This story relates to a commercial property, but the principles remain the same for residential property.

Commercial loans can be a little more complicated than residential loans and have a lot more variability. Lenders generally want an LVR of 60 to 70 per cent and a short loan term, such as to match the lease length, which can be five or even ten years; but, as we noted above, sometimes this can change. My property was with Westpac at about 50 per cent LVR and was valued at $640,000 with a $320,000 loan, and the loan term was going to run out with my tenant's lease after about 1.5 years. This meant that, though I was not in a rush to refinance, I was certainly keeping my eyes and ears open for different opportunities in the market. This is when I learnt that ANZ had created a new facility that would accept an 80 per cent LVR on a 30-year term for any commercial lend below $1 million. I took my loan to ANZ, and they valued my property at $800,000 and increased my loan amount to $640,000, which meant that I could take out that additional $320,000 equity as a loan and reinvest it. I ended up buying a share of another property that gave me an 8.25 per cent net yield, increasing my passive income by $26,400 annually.

The finance can make or break a property deal. As the markets change, you need to keep a close eye on what lenders are doing because it may mean that you can take advantage of different facilities to improve your position. Also, paying attention to the banks will give you strong cues as to how the market is performing. When the banks are loosening up and allowing the money to flow, you can expect people to start buying property; when the banks start to get tight, that's when the property market will likely contract.

How to not f*ck it up

The APRA and the RBA make regular long-winded announcements about the economy, finance and how they see things playing out in the market. Every month the RBA will announce the cash rate and comment on whether it is going up, down or staying the same, and why. When you are just starting out, this might be all a bit much, but as you get used to the jargon it can be very helpful for understanding the current state of the market and helping you predict what's going to happen.

However, a much easier way to get your information is via banks or, my preferred way, mortgage brokers. Mortgage brokers are great because they talk to all the banks and know their appetites for different loans. For instance, a broker may tell you that the major banks are only interested in P&I loans for owner-occupiers and will charge a premium for IO loans. They will also be able to tell you about changes to credit policy around the debt-to-income ratios, for example, or changes to how much rent banks will accept as part of your servicing income.

Mortgage brokers and banks cannot charge you a fee without telling you in advance, and the vast majority do not charge fees unless you have successfully settled a loan. So, do not be afraid to reach out to a few and have some productive conversations.

Government policy

I bought my first property at 22 years old after the New South Wales government announced that it was going to change the First Home Owner Grant (FHOG) to remove the $10,000 bonus and the stamp duty concession from all pre-existing real estate.

With this huge change about to take place, people flooded the market to snap up real estate below the $600,000 FHOG limit, causing a sharp increase in price at the bottom end of the market. This is a normal human response to government policy. When we see or hear about an opportunity to make money or benefit from an incentive, we react. This is why it is so important to pay attention to what the government is saying about property and finance.

I bought a two-bedroom apartment in the south-west Sydney suburb of Lakemba for $236,000 and over 12 months its value grew to more than $320,000. I had put in $18,900 and the property had grown by $84,000 in just one year. I was over the moon because it would have taken me more than five years to save that amount.

Here are a few questions to find answers to before you buy your next property:

- What are the current government incentives?
- What government incentives are being discussed?
- What are the current laws around real estate and are there any proposals for them to change?

Like any game, the rules are what determine what moves people will make. For instance, in Monopoly you can only start buying after you go around the board once; so, as soon as people get around the board that first time, the buying frenzy begins! Government policy is the same: the game has rules, so when there are changes there will always be people who look to take advantage of those changes. Therefore, understanding the implications of policy changes will help you understand how people's behaviour and the demand for real estate in the market will change.

How to not f*ck it up

Reading government policy is not the most exciting of activities but it is the most reliable way to learn about the market and what is available to you. However, there are a few ways to learn about these changes without reading the policy docs:

- *Newspapers:* All the major news publications will generally cover changes to government policy, particularly when they affect the real estate market. Staying across the headlines is a good way to maintain a top-down view of the market. You can count on these publications to give a quick snapshot of what policy changes are being suggested and, eventually, implemented. Newspapers will generally also have an opinion about the impact and should link to where the information has come from.

- *Solicitors and conveyancers:* Your legal representation should understand the changes that are being implemented in the law. They may know what changes are being suggested by the government and should definitely know what the current rules and regulations are. However, there may be occasions when they do not, which is why it is important for you to at least have a general understanding of what is happening. If you are buying a property and there is free money available to you, I would hate for you to miss out on it.

- *Agents:* There are different types of real estate agents both buying and selling property on behalf of their clients. There are local sales agents, who work on behalf of vendors (property owners), and buyers agents and investment agents, who work for the buyers.

Each of these agents will generally know about the different types of government policy affecting their market. They're a great, quick source of information about what impacts the different incentives are having, and it does not cost you anything to talk to them. However, the reliability of their information may be a little shaky. It's best to have a chat and learn broadly what's available but then do your own research.

· *Financial planners and accountants:* As with agents, financial planners and accountants will generally know what's happening in the market since it impacts their clients and the work they do. However, it is best to qualify the information you learn from them yourself.

In short, while all of these professionals will be able to help and give you guidance, there is no substitute for reading the primary information for yourself, because that way no details will slip through the gaps. These little mistakes could cost you tens of thousands of dollars and potentially lead you to miss seeing trends that are likely to occur as a result of upcoming changes. So, it pays to stay well informed, even just at the top level. You can also learn about the details as they become relevant.

Sentiment

Do people feel that the property market is going to rise or fall in the foreseeable future? This is market sentiment, and it determines how people will behave when they are buying and selling.

Market sentiment is the view or opinion that is held or expressed by the public. It is how your friends, family, colleagues, media, real estate agents and government see the economy and real estate market. What they are saying at the barbeque or around the water cooler will help to inform you whether it is a buyers' or a sellers' market currently. This helps you understand who has the perceived power in the negotiation over your next property purchase. Market sentiment is an important consideration when judging whether to enter the market or hold off – or, as discussed earlier, to move fast in a negotiation or drag it out.

Market sentiment is affected by many factors. As discussed previously, interest rates and government policy are big levers that impact the market and how people feel about whether it is going to rise or fall. Economic conditions such as the inflation rate, the job market and gross domestic product (GDP) growth are all indications of how the market is performing. Then there are global events such as wars, and black swan events such as COVID-19, that impact how people feel about the market and whether they want to get in or stay out.

Generally speaking, when the property market is rising, there is a positive outlook, and that is when people want to get in and ride the wave. When the market is falling, the outlook is negative, and people want to get out or hold off purchasing. This makes sense to a point, but you should really be behaving in the opposite way.

When your favourite shops put up signs advertising 50 per cent off for the end of financial year sales or Black Friday deals, do you run away or run inside? To quote the famous investor Warren Buffett, 'Be fearful when others are greedy and greedy when others are fearful'. Moving separately from the herd is one of the best ways to find greener pastures and make great profits.

Now, I don't want to make things more complicated than necessary, but there is a difference between general market sentiment and specific market sentiment (which changes from one area to the next). The general property market may be performing poorly but select councils and suburbs may be on the rise. This can come down to local dynamics such as infrastructure projects, affordability or supply, or the area can simply be a blue-chip location that people desire and where the locals do not need to discount.

Here are a few questions to ask to help you understand market sentiment:

- Is the market running hot and are prices inflated?
- Are people scared about the future and uncertain about what will happen next?
- What are people buying and what is their motivation? (Are they homeowners or investors?)
- Is the mass market movement a true indication of what is happening and can I take advantage of it?

How to not f*ck it up

The simple solution here is to read some newspapers and websites and talk to people. Reading the news will give you an insight into how economists and industry people are seeing the property market. The news will often be sensationalised and point to the potential market extremes, since this is what sells, but this is still useful information because this feeds market sentiment.

Often the best way to gauge accurate local market sentiment is to talk to local real estate agents. They are at the forefront of the property market, talking to sellers and potential buyers every day. I have found that, despite the fear that all agents are commission-hungry liars, they are generally up-front about what they are experiencing. If times are quiet or busy, they will let you know; if the vendor is eager to sell or happy to hold off, they are going to say this too.

Here are some email subscriptions I use for market insights:

- Herron Todd White's Month in Review
- The Urban Developer

- Cushman & Wakefield
- Domain
- Realestate.com.au
- CoreLogic's Monthly Housing Chart Pack.

I don't believe in trying to time the real estate market, but it pays to have an understanding of the market sentiment, since this will determine how you are going to behave once you decide to buy.

Chapter 2

People

Understanding people and their behaviour is extremely important when investing in real estate. At the end of the day, you are buying the property for them. You need to have the end in mind and really consider who is likely to rent or buy the property you intend on investing in. It is also important to look at who your neighbours are and think about how they might change over time, as this is a good indication of how a market will likely change.

To be a good investor it is extremely helpful to take an interest in demographics and learn about people's behaviours and tastes today, as well keeping in mind how they might change and develop in the future.

So, what do we want to know about people?

- *Demographics:* age, ethnicity, occupation, religion, income
- *How they travel:* by car, walking, by public transport
- *What the average household looks like:* size, marital status, family composition.

Discovering this information is important because it will tell you who makes up the market. Then you can predict what types of property these people will want and how the market is likely to change over time.

Demographics

Looking into the demographic profile of a market will tell you about who is living there. After diving into the details, you can make predictions about their tastes and preferences: how they like to live and what's important to them. If you understand their preferences, then you are better able to pick a property that will always be tenanted and is likely to grow in value.

Age

How old are the people in the area? It is very important to learn if the market is full of families, pre-retirees, retirees, students or young adults. Members of each group like to live differently and have different requirements of their homes and lifestyles. Families like larger homes with space, storage and ideally a bit of grass. Pre-retirees and retirees like homes all on one level with few to no stairs, as well as convenience and low maintenance. Students and young adults want to be close to the action, with limited maintenance and a space that they can easily share.

These are only generalisations and surface-level observations, but they can be very helpful when you consider what might be important to your target market.

Ethnicity and religion

Learning about people's ethnicities and religions provides a view into their culture and how they like to live. People from different cultures come to Australia with varying values systems, and these values systems determine the types of properties they want to rent and eventually buy. For instance, many Chinese people value proximity to the city, train stations, shops and amenities, and are very happy to purchase apartments for all this convenience. On the other hand, while Indian and Pakistani people value convenience, they generally value land above all else. These are obviously generalisations, but they can be telling.

Another important factor is that migrants will often gravitate towards their ethnic group for comfort, support and nostalgia. This means that you can reliably predict the flow of people into different areas based on their ethnicity. For instance, from the 1950s to the 1970s many Italians who immigrated to Australia moved into specific areas, such Carlton in Melbourne and Leichhardt in Sydney. This is important information since you can read the census and see which migrant groups are entering the country, look at where they are likely to move to and get ahead of the demand for a location, then make an investment and watch it grow.

Occupation and income

Occupation and income statistics offer a great perspective on how an area is changing over time. This information will tell you how much disposable income households have and whether a suburb is gentrifying. 'Gentrification' is a fancy word for the process of wealthier people moving into a poor urban area, improving housing and attracting new businesses. On paper, this is indicated by incomes in the area are going up; on the street it is evidenced by new cafes, bars and restaurants, and richer people walking around with little fluffy dogs. Investing in gentrifying areas is a great way to ensure capital growth, because the area has the attention of people with high incomes who are willing to spend more of their money on buying, improving and renting properties there.

Travel

How people get to places of work, fun and relaxation is an important consideration when buying property. This information will inform you about what is important to them to live comfortably. Each market has different requirements for parking and access to amenity: in some markets, car spaces or garages are a must-have and properties without them will not grow in value or rent out anywhere near as quickly as their neighbours, whereas in others they are of lesser importance (but still a bonus) if the property is close to public transport and local amenities.

The average household

Understanding the composition and marital status of people in the average household gives you an insight into the specific types of property in demand in that market. Are there more families, couples or single people moving into the area? As mentioned, each group has a different way of living and different demands for the type of homes they want to rent or buy. An increase in dual income, no kids couples moving to an area generally means higher average disposable incomes and a growing demand for convenience and smaller spaces. More families moving in means a demand for more space, more rooms and bigger backyards.

Who is likely to rent your property?

Before you buy an investment property, you will want to know who you're likely to rent it to. It is extremely helpful to understand how much demand there will be for your investment today and in the future. If you understand your target market and have bought an investment with all the right features, you will find it easy to rent it out and keep increasing the rent over time.

For example, let's consider who might rent a city-fringe two-bedroom apartment. There are two main reasons why people rent an apartment: affordability and convenience. So, with this in mind, depending on the market rent in the area and the local amenities, you can start piecing the puzzle together. People who might rent this property include:

- a dual income, no kids couple
- a single person who takes the head lease and sublets the other room
- downsizers who have moved out of a house and want the flexibility of something smaller
- friends who each take a room and halve the rent between them
- a small family – a couple with a baby or even a couple of young kids, who are looking to eventually move into something bigger
- a single mum or dad
- a wealthy executive who wants the extra space.

A two-bedroom apartment is the most versatile rental property with the largest group of potential investors. Within each of the broad categories above there are opportunities to go even deeper by exploring the specifics of who these people are, what is important to them and what they will pay a premium for.

Who is likely to buy your property?

You may not ever want to sell your home or investment property, but that doesn't mean you don't want there to be a strong demand for it. A strong demand for your property means that its value will grow, giving you equity that you can use over time. When you have a firm grasp of the demographics in an area and the locals' lifestyles, you know exactly who you are marketing to and what their tastes are. This empowers you to make good decisions about what property you will buy and therefore know who will want to pay a premium for it if you choose to sell. To put it simply, it is about learning what is demanded by the local population and then giving it to them.

Case study: buying my second property

To illustrate, here's how I made $121,000 in three years with only a $5000 deposit by buying what people were saying was a terrible investment.

On paper I can see why people had this opinion: it was a one-bed, one-bath, no-car apartment in Newcastle. I was 23 years old and this was my second property, so I did not have a lot of savings and my borrowing capacity was limited because my income was still growing, which meant that I had a limited budget. So, I had three choices: I could push my finances to the limit and put a lot of stress and pressure on myself by buying a two-bedroom apartment; I could wait and save for a few more years; or I could buy this one-bedroom apartment.

I had done a lot of research into the local property market, and I could see that Newcastle's CBD was changing rapidly. There was investment going into the city, making it a much nicer place to live, and I could also see a significant change in the kinds of people moving in. There were two big groups of people moving into the CBD: young professionals and pre-retirees. Both groups had good disposable income and wanted similar things from city living: convenient nightlife and close proximity to the beaches. I knew that the older demographic of pre-retirees and right-sizers (people moving from large homes into smaller ones) wanted to live in apartments but that the transition could be difficult, so they liked plenty of space on one level.

Knowing all this, let's dive into the details of what I liked about this one-bedroom apartment. Yes, it was only 50 square metres internally and did not have a car space, but it had a massive 50-square-metre balcony, and the development was in the heart of the east end of the city and only a five-minute walk to the beach. I felt that these two factors more than compensated for the property's shortcomings. It was not perfect, but I felt that the good outweighed the bad, and I just needed the investment to be good enough to make me money.

I decided to go ahead with the investment. I negotiated with the developer and, since the market was weak at that point in time, I was able to get away with only putting down a $5000 deposit. The property took two years to be completed off the plan and I held onto it for another 12 months for tax purposes. (If you hold your investment for more than 12 months, you only need to pay capital gains tax on the 50 per cent of the uplift – the gain you have made above the original purchase price less your costs, including investments you've made into the property through upgrades and so on.)

I bought this property for $298,000 and sold it for $410,000 to a right-sizer couple who wanted that extra space and convenience. I made $121,000 off that investment and was able to use the profit to buy a bigger, two-bedroom apartment in the city.

The interesting thing about this story is that a couple years after I bought this apartment I saw a similar opportunity in the same city. This property had one bedroom, one bathroom and one car space, and it was 52 square metres internally with 40 square metres of external space. I was helping a client with a limited budget, and I suggested that we use the same strategy. They bought the property for $350,000 and ended up selling it to a right-sizer for $450,000 two years later.

These are great examples of targeted market fit and being able to make a good sum of money off what most people would call bad investments. Many people would pass on these properties in favour of waiting and saving more money. However, in both instances, there is no way that the investor (myself or my client) would have been able to save that $100,000 in the two to three years in which they made that profit. In both cases, the property ended up being a great stepping stone to eventually buying something bigger and better.

How to not f*ck it up

The simple solution here is to keep your eyes open as you are exploring the new area where you want to buy. Take note of who is walking around the area: at the local shops, the train station and so on. Also, talk to property managers and sales agents. Property managers spend all their time leasing out properties to the local market and sales agents are on the front line with both buyers and sellers. You will learn a lot from both.

To get a deeper understanding of a market's demographics, you will need to do a bit of research. This can be difficult but, with a little time and dedication, you will soon learn to notice what's important in the data. Looking at data for one year will show you how things are today, but it is by comparing one year to previous years that you will see the changes.

If you would like to do your own research, .id (home.id.com.au) – 'the population experts' – is a great resource that provides insights into populations. Also, the Australian Bureau of Statistics (ABS) is for all you statisticians out there who want the raw data: abs.gov.au/census/find-census-data/quickstats/2021/AUS.

Chapter 3

Infrastructure

It is important to know what infrastructure projects are being planned for an area, because this will highlight possible future opportunities and, in turn, act as the road map for how a market is going to change and improve over time. Allow me to illustrate this with another case study.

Case study: my second investment property in Newcastle

In 2014 I was working as the head of sales at a development company and doing a lot of research into the city of Newcastle. A few years earlier I had bought an apartment there (as discussed in chapter 2), and I could see there was still a lot of potential for growth in the city. So, going against popular opinion, I decided to put down a 5 per cent deposit on an apartment west of Newcastle's CBD with two bedrooms, two bathrooms and one car space. The property was selling for $460,000 and was in front of a decommissioned heavy railway line. Newcastle council had approved plans to end the heavy rail line and create a brand new central station about 150 metres from the development. From the new train station, you could catch an express to Sydney or all stops through Newcastle. The council had also approved plans to create a new bus terminal, along with a light rail that would run through Newcastle and stop just before the main beach.

As an investor this was all music to my ears because I could see that, when this was all completed, the apartment I had just bought would be close to a transport node important to many people who want to easily commute to Sydney, around the city and to the beach. Newcastle council had government funding and state budget support to enrich the CBD and had released plans showing their intention to revive the city along the new light rail line to encourage nightlife, culture and the arts. Furthermore, there were plans for a brand new university campus and for large chunks of land to be redeveloped over time from ugly car parks, ports and light industrial buildings into walkways, green spaces and new commercial and residential buildings.

Since the city was investing in itself, it was also attracting a lot of private investment from people and businesses who shared the vision for the city that the council was selling. Reading all of these approved and proposed plans, it became clear to me that Newcastle was on the rise and that this particular area, Wickham and Newcastle West, had the most to gain from the coming changes. This part of the city was going to change from a light industrial, lifeless area to a central hub full of transport infrastructure, retail stores and culture. Fundamentally, the western part of the city was going to become a much nicer place to live in time.

Six years after I bought my property in this neighbourhood, it was clear that I was not only correct but had actually underestimated how much the city would change. It now has world-class hotels, bars and restaurants that rival Sydney's. That two-bedroom apartment had very little vacancy and was positively geared, so it was making me money every year. When I eventually decided to sell it in 2022 to make some cash available to buy another property, I got $750,000 for it, making me $290,000.

This is a great example of the benefits of paying attention to the research, drawing conclusions about the future and allowing the property market to do all the work for you.

*

When assessing infrastructure, you need to ask yourself four key questions:

1. What is there today?
2. What is coming and how will people's lives be improved?
3. Where is it going?
4. When will it be completed?

What is there today?

When assessing a market and its long-term investment trajectory, it is important to have a good understanding of the infrastructure servicing the local population. Broadly speaking, there are 16 different types of infrastructure: aviation, bridges, dams, drinking water, energy, hazardous waste, inland waterways, levees, parks and recreation, ports, rail, roads, schools, solid waste, transit and wastewater. All of these types of infrastructure are critical for building cities and a thriving population, but you certainly do not want all of these services on your doorstep. Proximity to these services can have a dramatic impact on the price of property and determine its value in the market today and in the future.

The suburbs surrounding Sydney Park in Sydney's inner west provide a good example of this. From about 1870 to 1950 the area was used to create bricks; then, from 1950 to the late 1970s, it became a dumping ground for much of Sydney's waste. During these years the area was home to the working class and was not a desirable place to live. However, after the transformation of the dump into an award-winning park, the inner western suburbs began to thrive.

When canvassing a new area to invest in, pay close attention to any existing infrastructure that is noisy, smelly or dangerous, as this will generally bring down the value of property in the area and put a ceiling on the price that you can achieve in the future. Roads, trains and schools can be exceptions to this: they are all loud, and the first two can impact air quality, but they can all have a positive impact on prices. It just comes down to the proximity of each particular property to these types of infrastructure. The ideal distance is close enough that you can enjoy the convenience but not so close that they become a daily irritation.

What is coming and how will people's lives be improved?

What infrastructure is coming to an area is only as important as the impact it will have on people's lives. This is where all the potential value is created. Planned infrastructure projects provide a window to the future and, depending on what is going to be delivered, will determine the long-term impact on property prices. As with current infrastructure, not all planned infrastructure is favourable: some will have a negative impact depending on what it is and how close it is to your property.

When looking at what is to come and how the local population's lives will be affected, I think about two key factors: amenity (something people will use) and accessibility (something that makes travel faster or more convenient).

Amenity

The delivery of new amenities is exciting for a suburb because they bring value and utility. Following are a few examples of different types of amenities and the value that they bring.

Educational facilities such as schools, TAFEs, universities and colleges are great value-creating amenities because they bring jobs and provide a very important service. Studies have shown that proximity to schools can have a significant impact on property prices. Buyers are willing to pay 26 per cent more for properties in the catchment areas of highly ranked primary schools and 8 per cent more for moderately ranked primary schools. Prices for properties within highly ranked secondary schools' catchment areas are 11 per cent higher, and rents are up to 9 per cent higher. TAFEs, colleges and universities attract students, who are potential tenants and bring a vibrant energy to a location as well as retail spending.

People love to let their hair down, relax and enjoy themselves. Cinemas, arcades and music facilities are all examples of urban activation that enhance culture and lifestyle, providing **arts and recreation** options that give residents something to do in their spare time. They create jobs and are usually around retail centres, and they lift the value of real estate because people actively search them out. They attract a broad range of people from all demographic groups – from young singles to families to older retirees.

Shops, bars, cafes and restaurants are very good examples of amenities that can increase the value of real estate in a location. Generally speaking, the better the retail offering in an area, the higher property prices will be. **Retail trade** creates job opportunities, attracts people and stimulates lifestyle; people of almost all demographics will pay a premium to live close to the conveniences that retail trade brings. Retail trade also brings in visitors from neighbouring suburbs, driving demand further as more people are exposed to the local culture. Paying attention to the changes in retail trade can be significant: new retail precincts will often have an immediate impact on an area, but a shift in the quality of the offering is also a great sign of gentrification and changing values and demographics. These shops, cafes and restaurants only pop up if there's a demand and stay if the local population can afford to service them.

New **parks, green spaces and sporting facilities** are a great driver of demand. People are always looking for spaces where they can unwind, walk their dogs, play with their kids and keep fit. These types of facilities became especially popular after COVID-19. Unlike some other amenities where you want to be close but not too close, generally people are happy to be very close to parks and green spaces. Sporting facilities can be different, but this just depends on their size and the noise that they create.

Health care services are great for job creation and also draw potential buyers and tenants. Health care professionals place great value on living close to work because doing shift work and being on call makes it difficult for them to live too far away.

Accessibility

There are several ways that local, state and federal governments can improve accessibility. This new infrastructure, depending on its size, can cost hundreds of millions or even billions of dollars and take many years to deliver or can be small-scale and delivered at a local level. New means of transportation generally equate to faster or more convenient commutes, which is a big driver of property prices. They can represent a boost to economic activity during their delivery but also after their completion.

As I've stated many times already, people pay for convenience. If you have ever been to an amusement park that sells a 'fast pass', you will understand. If you have never bought a fast pass, the next time you have the option to I very much recommend it. Rather than standing in queues for 30 minutes to an hour each time, you simply walk to the front of the queue for every ride and get the most out of your day. People value their time; it is the one thing you cannot get more of, but you can definitely save it, especially when commuting in major cities.

Each of the following has its own impact on the property market through the creation of jobs while being delivered and, for some, long after completion.

Road networks can be very contentious, and are generally large in scale and take years to deliver. They can be smaller revamps of an existing network or huge, multistage motorways that span many suburbs and require tunnels and bridges. The bigger the infrastructure, the more contentious it is and the more time is required to complete it. Roads can have either negative or positive impacts on property values depending on proximity. Neighbouring a major motorway will put downward pressure on prices due to the noise, smell and pollution. However, if you are lucky enough to buy a property that is far enough away not to be negatively impacted but also conveniently close enough to the exit or entry point, this can be very valuable because of reduced travel times.

New **public transport** infrastructure, such as for buses, light rail and trains, can be divisive in communities – as can any new infrastructure project – but they are generally received more favourably because they have an immediate positive impact for everyone. New bus stops and an increase in services are pretty small additions and fast to bring in, but they are localised and have a pretty small impact on property prices. The addition of metro, light rails and heavy rail stations and lines all have hugely positive impacts on real estate pricing. Train stations take years of planning and then building before they are delivered but, once completed, they have the power to transform a location. They give people better access to work and leisure and have the added benefit of bringing people together. Having people enter and exit one location can also attrawct retail or commercial trade, depending on council rezoning of land around the station. This new flurry of activity can have the flow-on effect of helping to gentrify a location.

Airports and marinas are truly transformative pieces of infrastructure that can take decades to get approved and funded, and they are typically massive projects. They generate lots of jobs on site both while under construction and after completion, but they also create just as many if not more jobs around the site through ancillary and complementary services.

For example, airports are a focal point for tourism and commercial trade. Tourists need car hire, food and accommodation. Commercial trade requires logistics hubs, which have storage and transport facilities to take the goods from the planes and move them around the country. Further to this, depending on the size of the airport, you may have military operations, education and health care facilities, and commercially zoned land that allows for retail trade and office operations. All of these services represent economic activity and, most importantly, jobs.

These types of operations take time to develop and mature – they take place over the course of a decade or longer – so it is the patient investor who wins here. However, since it is well known that this type of infrastructure brings so much value, it is common to see land values in the location start to climb even before construction starts, let alone finishes. A perfect example of this is the airport that is being built (at the time of writing) in the south-west of Sydney in Badgerys

Creek; soon after the government approved the airport, land values skyrocketed and local landowners became millionaires practically overnight.

It is not just large-scale works that impact on property prices: little local projects such as new **walkways and cycling paths** can have a big impact. It is often these little, intimate details that make a suburb a better place to live. We all love being able to get to our local amenities easily. These are small projects that can easily go unnoticed, but their impact is immediate. Being able to travel around the streets, cross major highways and access parks, shops and public transport more safely and conveniently improves the locals' quality of life and drives up real estate values in the area.

Where is it going?

Where a project will be delivered is as important as what it is. The details matter, and sometimes it can be difficult to accurately read the approved plans. General understanding is enough to allow you to buy strategic pieces of real estate, but understanding the details will help you avoid buying in a spot that may be negatively affected. Depending on what you are buying, this may mean avoiding noise and air pollution or an interrupted view.

When investing in property in regional cities, new suburbs or an area that's getting an overhaul, be mindful of the concentration of new projects. To achieve the biggest growth in value you ideally want to identify a concentration of infrastructure. Generally, the more that is being spent in a specific location, the better, though the impact of this spending is the more accurate indicator of future demand. It stands to reason that the greater the number of infrastructure projects that are planned in a concentrated area is, the greater the impact on the area will be.

When will it be completed?

Once you know what infrastructure projects are coming, it is important to pay attention to who is spending the money and when each project is due to be completed. The announcement of a project will cause a stir, and there may be some early price growth depending on the size and potential impact of the investment; however, investors at this stage are taking a big punt, so there may not be that much movement in the market.

The bigger price rise comes after the project is approved and confirmed to be delivered. At this point in time, you will see mostly investors moving into the market, speculating on the impact the project will have. Generally, homeowners are not interested because they will not yet be able to use the benefit. There may be some buying activity from investors while the project is under construction, but most buyers will be deterred by the noise, dust and commotion. A property's proximity to the project will affect the amount of rent that the investor will receive or the homeowner's quality of life. The last stage of growth comes upon completion of the project, years after the utility is first announced. Now that it is actively improving people's lives, this is when the largest group of buyers enters the market as homeowners look to enjoy the benefits.

Here's a hypothetical example: a government approves and funds a train station that's due to be completed in three years' time. We're confident in the funding of the project because it's coming from the government, and we know that the completed station will reduce people's travel times and improve their quality of life, increasing the demand to live in the area. So, we can clearly identify this key piece of infrastructure as a growth driver that will impact the area on and after a specific date.

This is exactly what I experienced with the properties I bought in Newcastle. The announcement of the construction of a light rail line through the city brought a lot of media attention, but it was not yet widely accepted in the community. It was a proposal, but it had not yet been approved. I noticed that there was some activity in the property market, but not a lot, because at this point it was just speculation whether the light rail line would be built or not.

When it was formally approved, things changed, though not as dramatically as you would expect. Most of the activity came from developers and commercial investors looking to take advantage of the infrastructure to deliver large-scale projects for homeowners. People generally do not appreciate the extent of the impact that an infrastructure project will bring, because most people do not pay much attention to this kind of reporting.

While the rail line was under construction, the city was a mess. There were tradespeople everywhere, as well as trucks and heavy machinery making noise and spreading dust all over the place. The city was not a desirable place to live, which negatively impacted rents and property prices.

After the project was completed, prices stabilised, and this is when property prices and rents started to experience growth. Now it was beneficial to live close to the light rail because it made it easy to get to the beach and there were new bars, cafes and restaurants opening up all along the line.

How to not f*ck it up

Planning around new infrastructure projects requires deliberate thinking and the ability to think ahead to empathise with future homeowners. It requires you to collate as much information as possible, verify it and then put all the pieces together to see what grand vision of the future the infrastructure creates. Most people do not take the time to do this and struggle to see beyond what is here today.

While the light rail line was being built, I would often take my clients out to see the proposed sites to explain the master plan and paint a grand vision for the future. This grand vision was hard to see when we were looking at abandoned school buses, run-down warehouses and a group of local chickens that would periodically walk up and down the street.

Here are the tools and sources that I use to learn about infrastructure timing and delivery:

- *Google Alerts (google.com.au/alerts):* This tool will be your best friend. You simply put in the keywords you want to keep track of – for example, 'Melbourne infrastructure' – and whenever a new release comes out, you'll know about it.

- *Government planning portals:* These are really good places to learn well ahead of everyone else what's being planned, what's changing and what's coming to the market. A full list of planning portals for each state and territory can be found at the back of this book.

- *Budgets:* Paying attention to the federal and state budgets is always a good idea. These are the most obvious indicators of big-ticket items coming to states and cities.

- *News:* Reading the good old newspaper and subscribing to different news sources is a great way to keep on top of new projects coming to the market.

Governments produce reports highlighting their plans for the next 20 to 30 years. They make predictions about population growth and need to consider health care, education, employment opportunities, travel times and leisure options. With all this information, they plan and map out where there will be clusters of population growth and where the infrastructure servicing them will be. The answer to where you could buy your next property is often laid out for you if you are willing to do the research and make the sacrifices to buy in these locations.

Chapter 4

Employment

No one likes to spend an hour or more commuting: waiting in traffic, sitting next to people on the bus or train or having to walk long distances to get to work. Generally, people will accept a 30-minute commute, but any more than that and it had better be for only a few days a week or it gets very tedious very quickly. As mentioned previously, people pay a premium for convenience and, when it comes to work – their source of income and family wellbeing – they will pay more to live nearby.

People do not usually think about this when looking to buy a property in a major metropolitan hub. They often take it for granted that whatever they buy in cities will be close to some kind of work for professionals, tradespeople or retailers. This is true, but cities are continually rezoning land and investing in themselves, which presents opportunities for property buyers.

If you are looking to invest outside of a major metro hub, you can get into a lot of trouble if you don't properly consider employment opportunities. Regional cities can provide great investment opportunities – they are affordable and offer excellent yields and, if you pick the right town, you can also ride some good growth – but, if you are not careful, you can just as easily lose all that you have invested.

Here is an extreme example of the impact that employment opportunities can have on the price of real estate. Around 2014 Australia went through a huge mining boom. Miners were getting paid large sums of money to fly in to work at a mine and then fly out to their homes for rest. While in these towns, they paid huge rents, because there were few available properties and they had the income to pay whatever was needed to get a home. Many Australian country towns saw their property prices jump 30, 40 or even 50 per cent overnight. In central Queensland, about 12 hours from Brisbane, a town called Moranbah has a population of about 8000 people and the major employer is the local mine. At the peak of the mining boom, you could buy a fully renovated four-bedroom house for $820,000 and rent it out for $1600 per week. Months later you would have been hard-pressed to rent out the property for more than $400 per week, and that same house would sell for $170,000. This was because the price of resources dropped, the major employer terminated contracts and there was no one left to rent these properties for crazy prices, and investors were left with terrible investments.

When determining the long-term success and viability of almost all real estate markets – from city fringes to small towns to urban apartment complexes – you need to consider diversification (what are the main sources of employment?) and travel time (how long will it take to commute there?).

Diversification

Diverse employment opportunities are available in major metro hubs around Australia, so employment opportunities are not much of a concern in those areas. However, one of the main traps that people fall into when looking for an 'affordable market' is to pick a rural town that is reliant on one sole industry, or even a single commodity. If that commodity begins to fail, so too does the workforce; and if there's a mass exodus of these renters, then that will be a *big* problem in that market.

Fortunately, the opposite of this is also true. Taking into account investments in infrastructure, the evolutions of cities and how they will grow can make you wildly successful.

As discussed previously, new schools, hospitals and retail centres – and roads and public transport infrastructure connected to these centres – present excellent opportunities. A solid future is ensured by a robust workforce that is supported by multiple employment options, such as:

- construction
- accommodation and food services
- transport and warehousing
- public administration
- education
- health care
- scientific and technical services
- information and media.

All these industries contribute to a vibrant local economy and workforce, meaning that the market is not reliant on any one industry to keep the population employed and prosperous. Good job opportunities and growing incomes are great for a local community because they give people more disposable income to spend on their homes.

Travel time

When governments make plans to cater for population growth and the happiness of citizens, they typically account for a 30-minute commute. Yes, people will often make the sacrifice of commuting longer distances, but 30 minutes is sustainable and within what the average person considers acceptable.

When considering the impact of new commercial precincts, industrial sites or retail centres on an area, they are likely to have a positive impact if they are within the 30-minute striking distance.

How to not f*ck it up

I have already noted some of the best resources for this information on diversification and travel time:

- .id (home.id.com.au) has a wealth of data that you can look into and read.
- ABS (abs.gov.au/census) is for all you statisticians out there who want the raw data.
- Local, state and federal government websites will have all this information freely available for you; just type your state and 'investment in infrastructure' into Google (e.g. 'NSW investment in infrastructure').

In summary, you want to consider if the place you are investing in has the economic opportunities to support the local population. Opportunities arise in locations where lots of jobs will be created and the quality of these jobs is getting better. The more money people have, the more they will spend, and one of the first things people often spend their money on is their home.

Chapter 5

Supply

Supply is one of the hardest forces to predict and get your head around. It will also be one of the biggest reasons why your property either experiences tremendous growth or none. A tightly held market that rarely has properties available for sale is likely to have strong growth potential, whereas the opposite is true for a market that often has a lot of properties available and new stock coming onto the market.

Judging the supply of new property coming onto the market can be done, but it is difficult without using expensive software, or spending a huge amount of time in local government databases reviewing approved plans and logging this information into a spreadsheet and then comparing this information with current supply levels and population data. Fortunately, there are several websites that will give you a sneak peek into this information, as well as primary resources that you can use to understand supply dynamics for yourself.

For the average homeowner or investor buying in an established market, supply can usually only become an issue with apartments, because it is very difficult to bring new houses and townhouses into an urban area since most places are already built out and there are no more open spaces to cut up into developable land. However, it is common for councils to make the zoning of real estate around train stations and business hubs higher density and allow for apartments to be created.

The other circumstance in which there may be a risk of too much new supply coming onto the market is when people are buying on the fringes of cities and in greenfield developments (where farms are cut up and turned into estates and subdivisions). There may be hundreds or thousands of properties that will be built in these developments and come onto the market over time.

Supply can also be an issue in a market where there is simply a lot of existing property for sale and long sales timelines. This has less to do with supply and more to do with the demand for property in the area. Nevertheless, this is good information to pay attention to because it gives you a read on what people want, how likely you are to see growth and, if you needed to exit the market, how long that would take.

Fortunately, this is not all bad news; new supply in a market can present opportunities. There are three main factors that determine this:

- *Timing:* When is the inbound supply arriving?
- *Type:* What types of properties are being developed?
- *Density:* Density equals intensity. This is a phrase I use to remind people that us humans love interaction with other humans, and so concentrations of people can be great for a property market.

Timing

As the saying goes, timing is everything. This is because it provides context to a situation and, in real estate, time in the market allows a community to mature, infrastructure to be completed and the population to grow.

If you have access to the data and want to do a deep analysis, you can predict the fluctuations of supply over time and compare this with forecasted population growth. This is valuable information that will provide an insight into market opportunities, such as a potential undersupply or oversupply of property over a given period. Though, as discussed, this type of analysis is difficult to do and not for everyone.

A much simpler way to analyse the impact of time on a market is to think about how much a market stands to change over longer periods of time. Most people fall into the trap of thinking about what is likely to happen over the space of months or a handful of years. The more important timescale to consider is a decade or more.

A bunch of new apartments, townhouses or houses coming into a market can present good buying opportunities, since this puts downward pressure on prices. Developers are under pressure to sell their stock relatively quickly and, when they have hundreds of properties to sell, they may be open to good discounts, incentives and upgrades. This is particularly true at the beginning of projects because the amount of supply coming onto the market is too much for demand to keep up with, so the price needs to go down in order for the properties to sell. This is a problem for prices locally over the short term but, after all the properties are developed, the market will find a new equilibrium and can go back to normal dynamics.

Typically, when the government plans new large-scale infrastructure such as commercial hubs, airports and train stations, they also plan for the population to grow and for the need to provide housing, so they make allowances for new supply to come into that market. They rezone land from commercial to residential, or rezone residential land from low-density houses to higher-density townhouses or apartments. Locations with transformative infrastructure may be perceived to have an oversupply of property coming to the market over the short term but, as a property owner, the bigger impact for you is the transformation of the area over the medium to long term.

Supply has an impact on prices but, if supply is met by demand and demand is likely to increase over time, you can use these forces to your advantage.

Type

When you have lots of similar properties available for sale or coming onto the market at once, this sends price growth backwards. The best example of this is apartment towers, which can contain thousands of properties that are all fundamentally the same in size, shape and amenity. They take a lot longer to grow in price than properties in other markets, which are varied and scarce.

However, lots of new supply does not necessarily mean prices will fall for all properties because it may create holes in the market: where there is a lot of one type of property, there may not be much of another. For example, if hundreds of one- and two-bedroom apartments come onto a market, the relative scarcity of three-bedroom apartments may mean that they become more expensive; or, if hundreds of new single-storey homes are built in an area on small blocks of land, double-storey homes with more land become standouts and may demand premium prices.

Let's revisit the story of my purchase of the one-bedroom Newcastle apartment (described in chapter 2). It was one of about 50 apartments in a development in Newcastle's CBD. The two big differences between mine and the many other apartments in the city of similar size, shape, amenity and quality were its position and the external balcony.

This little apartment was 500 metres from the beach, so people who loved the beach could walk there in minutes. It also had a 50-square-metre outdoor deck, meaning that the external space of the apartment was as big as the inside. This gave people choices: they could dress up the space with plants or put gym equipment, surfboards and bikes out there. At face value, this was just another apartment in a city full of apartments, but there were two big factors that made it unique, and this allowed me to sell it for a very strong profit after a short amount of time.

When assessing a property to buy, you want to make sure there are some defining characteristics that make your property unique relative to the other types of properties available in the market. Even if your intention is not to sell the property today, one day you might change your mind or want to extract equity. If your property is unique, this gives you the best chance of achieving growth and being unaffected by any potential new supply.

Density equals intensity

I lived in New York City in my mid-20s and then in London in my early 30s. Both are amazing cities with so much culture and many fun experiences to be had. They are some of the most expensive cities to live in and have some of the most expensive real estate in the world. They are expensive because of their access to high-quality economic opportunities, retail trade and dining and entertainment experiences. These cities have big populations and incredible density. With density brings intensity: noise, cars, buildings, cafes, bars and access to all things at all hours.

The more people there are living in a location, the more businesses pop up to service these people. As the incomes of these people increase over time, they demand a better lifestyle, and better businesses set up shop and thrive. With better quality offerings on the doorstep, the price of real estate in the area goes up.

Often, when people talk about density, it is with a sour face. The truth is that most people like density and the intensity that comes with it. People like cities because they like new experiences, novelty and other people. Density is not something to be scorned but, rather, appreciated.

When density is done right, it brings people together. It creates opportunities for entrepreneurs to express their creativity, which creates jobs and experiences. The next time you see a cluster of towers being built, you might think about them a little differently. Each of those buildings will be filled with people. All those people will be looking to spend money and create a home for themselves. These towers present opportunities for savvy investors who look to the future and think about how the area might change and what benefits the buildings will bring.

How to not f*ck it up

Finding out about the amount of supply in a particular market can be very difficult without spending lots of money or time. Here are some resources that you can use to either go into the granular detail (for a fee) or learn what you can without spending a cent:

- *Microburbs (microburbs.com.au):* Microburbs provides free, detailed scorecards on every address in Australia: sale prices, development applications, travel times, local amenities and more.
- *SQM Research (sqmresearch.com.au/index_property.php):* This is a good data provider for the property market.
- *DSR (dsrdata.com.au):* This is a good website for people who want to dive deep into suburbs' numbers. It offers a paid subscription

that allows you to see all of a suburb's key indicators, including yields, vacancy rates and much more.

- *SuburbTrends (suburbtrends.com):* This website covers a wide range of data for each suburb, such as growth scores, price rankings, vacancy rates, market summaries, market inventory trends, market listings volume trends, market median trends, rental price trends, rental vacancy rate trends, price segmentation and building approvals.

- *Cordell Connect (cordellconnect.com.au):* This is an expensive subscription that will give you full access to information on all the current developments coming to or currently in a market. It gives a very detailed view of the current market and future trends.

- *Government planning portals:* Each state and territory government has an online planning portal where you can look up development applications and permits that have been submitted to councils, as well as changes to zonings, which tells you when locations are changing their allowable heights, densities and commercial business practices. You can find the full list of websites at the back of this book.

- *Local councils:* Check your local council's website to see the current sites coming onto the market. (This can be a little time consuming.)

Here is a quick tip for the property nerds: a great indicator of the amount of supply versus demand is the sales ratio, which is the total number of properties on the market versus total number of sales per month. What you want to figure out is how long it would take for all the available properties in that market to be sold if no new properties were added. To do this, you can use all the sales from the past 12 months to calculate a rolling 12-month sales average and divide this by the total stock on the market. Property markets that have less than three months' worth of stock are generally considered tight markets and are likely to grow. There is a strong correlation between how long a market stays beneath the three-month mark and how fast prices go up.

Learning about the supply in the market gives you power over the market, whether you are buying a home or an investment. To do this, there are two websites that will become your best friends: domain. com.au and realestate.com.au. Be warned: this becomes extremely addictive and, if your significant other is already annoyed at you for checking your social media too much, they're going to have a new pet hate. At least this is for market research and a better future for you both, though!

What is being sold?

I like to kick off all my searches by filtering by what has been sold and narrowing it down to what is most relevant to me: just houses, for example. However, after you've looked at the last 12 months of sales at least, I would then widen the search to get a broader sense of what is being sold and how much of it is available, both in terms of neighbouring suburbs and different property types. You may notice that hundreds of two-bedroom units have been sold but not very many three-bedroom units, and perhaps even fewer houses. Also, keep an eye out for how big the properties are and get a sense for what would be seen as big or small in the area. This will equip you with the information you need to identify something unique when you are eventually ready to buy.

The aim of this search is to get a general sense of what type of real estate makes up most of the market and what the outliers are.

How much is property selling for?

When canvassing what is being sold, pay careful attention to the values. The sales made within the last three to six months are the most relevant, but there is value in looking at sales up to 12 months ago or more. When looking at the prices, take note of the different property features to see how they impact price and give yourself a better understanding of how the market values these features. Here's a list of property features to consider:

- *Size:* The size of the land, indoor space, balconies and backyard all have a big impact on price. All else being equal, the bigger the property is, the more expensive it will be.

- *Bedrooms:* The number of bedrooms and the size of each have a big impact on price. Generally, the more bedrooms there are, the more expensive the property will be, but you get diminishing returns past four. You want the bedrooms to be at least 2.8 metres by 2.8 metres: any smaller than this would be tight and almost wouldn't qualify as a bedroom.

- *Open space:* People love to have some open space so they can entertain, play with the kids or just hang out. The more of this there is, the better.

- *Privacy:* People value privacy. If a house, townhouse or apartment is overly exposed, this may decrease the value of the property. The opposite is also true.

- *Orientation:* Buyers value lots of natural light. Generally, people in the southern hemisphere like properties that face north because this means that the property will receive natural light all day. In Australia, this varies if the property is on the east or west coast since this affects whether the property has a water view. Also, people of some ethnicities value other orientations due to cultural preferences.

- *Elevation:* Properties with some elevation can demand a premium because they typically have few issues with flooding or water gathering. They may also benefit from a view, good airflow, natural light and privacy.

- *Parking spaces:* Having somewhere to park a car adds value to a property and can offer a premium depending on location. Though inner-city properties need parking spaces less, they are typically highly valued with these properties because they are less readily available. The value of the car park increases with the security that it provides: a lock-up spot is more valuable than an open space.

- *Materials:* That materials used to build a property have a big impact on its value. Whether it is made of double brick, brick veneer or some type of cladding impacts the perceived structural integrity, as well as sound and thermal insulation.

- *Location:* Where properties are located greatly affects their value, even from street to street. Is the property on a main road or a quiet cul-de-sac? Is it walking distance to any local amenities, such as the shops, park, train station or beach? Sometimes being close to all the action is not necessarily better because this can impact the security of the property and your peace and quiet. Location, location, location.

- *Floor plan:* I like to pay attention to a property's layout to see if it flows nicely. If you are a renovator then you are looking to see if there is potential to move walls, add bathrooms or create open spaces.

- *Age:* The age of a property has a big impact on the price. Newer properties cost more because they're ready to be lived in and generally have up-to-date fixtures, hardware and appliances. Newer properties are also typically better insulated from noise and heat. Old properties are great for picking up bargains and are often best if you are keen to get your hands dirty with a renovation.

- *Wet areas:* There is a lot of value in bathrooms and kitchens because these spaces are typically the hardest and most expensive to renovate. The value in these spaces is in the fixtures, appliances and hardware but also the space and positioning. More bathrooms and bigger kitchens point to higher prices.

· *Amenities:* More amenities generally mean more expense when running properties, whether they are apartment blocks, townhouse developments or houses, but they add lots of value. People appreciate access to a pool, gym, sauna or barbeque area.

· *Outlook:* Outlook can greatly change the value of a property. Whether it is of the city skyline, bush, beach or water, people generally like properties that look out on something rather than on other homes or a back fence.

· *Zoning:* If you are buying a house, the zoning of the land can impact the price significantly. Land that allows for higher-density accommodation will demand a premium because developers will be able to put townhouses on it, or potentially amalgamate a few blocks and build units.

Here's another quick tip for property nerds: the square metre rate is a good way to gauge value. To calculate it, take the price a property sold for and divide it by the size of the land (for houses) or internal space (for apartments). For example, if you have a 1000-square-metre block of land that has sold for $2 million, divide 2 million by 1000 to get 2000: the property sold for $2000 per square metre. The better the home is, the higher the rate will be, but you will also notice the rate fall for especially large properties. As a rule of thumb, the more work that needs to be done to the property, the cheaper it is likely to be, but also the bigger the opportunity there is to add value and create equity.

After you do this for enough properties in a suburb, you will see that the suburb fits within certain parameters, and you can use these to more accurately gauge whether you are getting a good deal or paying a premium for the property you want to buy. When helping my now-fiancée buy her first home, this was a great experience to help her learn the value of property in her target markets, and she went from being a complete novice to talking square metre rates with me when we were going shopping and making offers based on these figures.

How long does it take for property to sell?

The time it takes for a property to sell in a market is a good indicator of demand versus supply. Property markets in which properties take less than 30 days to sell would be considered tightly held. As a rule of thumb, the longer it takes for property to sell, the less likely you are to see growth. Paying attention to the speed of sales is helpful because it gives you a sense of the urgency in the market and how fast or slow you can move in that market.

This is what it means to look at the big picture while keeping an eye on some of the important details, understanding the big market forces that impact property prices and the implications that they will have over time. When buying your next property, a good view of the big picture will protect you from making some of the bigger mistakes that people commonly make. It will help you see the big problems to avoid so you don't f*ck it up.

*

Now we are going to dive into the details. I want to get you thinking like a local while teaching you about some of the technical details you will need so you can mitigate many of the risks you will face when buying a property.

PART II

The Details

The devil is in the details, and this is especially true when it comes to property!

I am not what most people would call a 'details' person but, when it comes to real estate, I have had to become one. Real estate is the single biggest discretionary purchase that most people will make. It is more expensive than a Ferrari, a Rolex, school fees or a big holiday. The size of this purchase – whether it is your own home or an investment – is huge and will leave a lasting impact on your life, for better or worse. This is why it is important to pay attention to the details so you do not f*ck it up.

In part I of the book, I explained what it was like for me buying my first property. This is a good case study into a lot of the things you can do wrong while still getting a property investment right.

I was 22 years old when I bought my first property. I knew that, with my savings and income at the time, I could not afford to buy anything for more than $250,000 and would need to use all the available government grants. At that stage there was a $10,000 bonus plus a full stamp-duty waiver for properties less than $600,000. With my budget set, I was looking to buy something as close to the city as possible, since I knew that I would also need to move into the property for 6 months within 12 months of purchasing it. This is how I ended up buying a two-bedroom apartment in Lakemba for $236,000.

However, it was not that simple. When taking a close look at the market, I noticed that there were a lot of units for sale and the prices varied significantly for reasons I did not yet understand. What I needed to do was get off the computer, put on my private investigator hat, hit the streets and gather a group of professionals around to me avoid f*cking up this first purchase.

Now that you have a good understanding of the big picture, it is time to zoom in and take a closer look at what you are about to buy. You need to get to know the neighbourhood, learn about all the local properties and pick a team of people to work for you so you have every chance of making the right decision.

By the end of this part of the book, it is my goal that you will have all the knowledge you need to feel confident when buying your next property. There are four main steps to picking your property:

1. Think like a local.
2. Understand different properties.
3. Pick your property.
4. Secure your investment.

Chapter 6

Think Like a Local

Locals can tell you where the best streets are, where to get the best coffee and when to avoid certain areas so you don't get stuck in traffic. They know why you would rather live on one street over another and can tell you how the suburb changes through the seasons. Locals have had the benefit of spending time in the area and have learnt many of the nuances that come with living there. They also have strong opinions on what constitutes a good or a bad buy when they see the prices that neighbours have sold their properties for.

In this chapter, we get our hands dirty and hit the streets to gain a deep, intimate understanding of the local market and what a good deal looks like. To do this, we need to explore two main topics: location and value.

Location

One of the best ways to learn about a market is to spend time there. Spend time driving around the area to get a sense of the distances between local amenities, and spend time walking the streets to get a better sense of the walkability of the area. If there are shops, cafes and amenities, take the time to sit, watch the world go by and enjoy what is there. If there are local parks, coastline walks or outdoor activities, immerse yourself in them and keep your eyes open for who's sharing in these experiences.

It is important to visit the area on different days and at different times of day to see how the traffic, noise and congestion vary during peak and off-peak hours. Develop a sense of what it would be like to live close to or further away from the local shops, churches and schools. All of this is valuable information about which streets you may want to buy in or avoid at all costs.

Real estate is a network asset. The property you buy is impacted by what is close by and, as the old saying goes for people, 'You are the average of the five people you hang around with most' – the same goes for property.

Case study: researching Lakemba

Lakemba was a very different area culturally to where I was living with my parents. The people were different to me in their religions, family structures and value systems. In order for me to better understand the area, I needed to think like a local.

While I was looking to buy my little Lakemba apartment, I paid attention to Google Maps to see what amenities there were locally and noted the price differences between streets. As I noted these differences, I visited properties for open house inspections and spoke to the agents about these differences. Over the course of about 90 days I developed an understanding that there was a strong Muslim community in the area and that they valued being close to their mosque, not far from the local school and less than a 10-minute walk to local shops. This narrowed down my search for this investment a lot.

While spending some time walking the streets, I also started to recognise that some streets were just nicer than others in their width and streetscape. Some felt leafy and green with wide footpaths and lots of houses, whereas others felt denser and had apartment buildings that were not very well maintained. All of this had an impact on pricing. Over time, I clarified which streets were better than others and where I needed to invest to benefit long term from good rents and strong capital growth.

How to not f*ck it up

When reviewing a location, I like to pay attention to the types of properties that are nearby and their general state of repair. Here are a few things to be mindful of:

- *Construction:* I am always mindful of work being done in the area. It's great to see homes being renovated, upgraded and built from the ground up. This tells me I am moving into an area that is experiencing growth; the people are houseproud and are driving up the value of the area by literally putting money into their house and the area.

- *Houseproud neighbours:* I like to see how the homes look from the street. Manicured lawns, beautiful landscaping and homes that are well maintained tell me that there are likely to be lots of owner-occupiers locally who take care of the properties. The opposite of this is also unfortunately true: homes that are not well maintained or have junk on their front lawns indicate that they may have renters or the owners don't care about the house. However, this indicates opportunity: areas with properties like this are typically cheaper to buy into.

- *Premium properties:* I always keep my eyes open for premium properties. It is great to see large, expensive homes in the street. They raise the value of the area and tell me that there is depth in the market, meaning that there are properties selling for high values, which lifts the ceiling of the value that I can achieve in the area if I were to ever sell.

Value

Locals have a very good sense of what constitutes good value in their area (even if they've been living there for years and are generally shocked by the prices of everything). An interested local will know what properties have sold for and which parts of their suburb will sell for more or less. They can point to the premium streets or the ones to avoid at all costs.

When buying in a new area, it is your job to know as much or more than the locals. Note the attributes of a suburb, such as the proximity to amenities, the fall of the land and the size and newness of the homes. Note the prices from previous sales. As discussed in chapter 5, you can use the price-per-square-metre calculation if you want to be a property nerd and get specific. Even if you don't go that deep, though, if you look at enough properties you should get a general sense of property values, and this will be helpful to you when you eventually choose to make an offer on a property.

A good way to gauge value is to find out what the median price of the suburb is and note whether the property you are buying is likely to be above or below this price. The median price is essentially the middle of the market, and you can find this value for all suburbs at either realestate.com.au or domain.com.au. Note the property's attributes and gauge a realistic price band – such as between $500,000 and $650,000 – and later verify this with the agents that hold the listing. Over time you will become more and more accurate.

After less than a month of looking, you will have a very good sense of price and value. After three months of looking at all the sales and properties on the market, you will likely know as much as the local real estate agent and be ready to negotiate a good deal.

When assessing the value of a property, do not get too hung up on price. This may sound like strange advice and you are probably thinking, 'Aren't they the same thing?' In my mind they are different. Price is what you pay, whereas value is what you receive. Lots of people will have an opinion on the price you pay without knowing about the value that you receive.

Here are some examples of what determines value:

- *Commercial value:* This relates to the commercial opportunity in an investment. The price you pay today is determined in part by the value you can create in the property over time. This may come from the property being part of a development or the fact that you can potentially add value via a subdivision or renovations. People may have opinions on the price you paid today, but they do not have full insight into the plans you have for the future.

- *Emotional value:* Paying above the asking price to secure a property for its emotional value is also a worthy cause. If the property is going to be your family home for years to come, if it is everything that you want and gives you space to grow and peace of mind, why not pay a little more than the asking price or what people expect? You cannot put a price on emotional and mental security. Paying a higher price for this security and investment in yourself can add tremendous value to your life.

- *Convenience:* Paying more for a property that saves you time and mental energy is money well spent. For example, if you buy a new property, friends, family and colleagues will have opinions and may say that you are making a terrible investment by paying a premium. However, while you may be paying more, you are receiving peace of mind in return and saving emotional energy and time. There is real value in buying a new property because everything is done for you – there is no additional work required. Also, if it is an investment, you get great tax benefits, better tenants and usually avoid the headaches of repairs and maintenance. A new property means you have more time for the other things in your life. Also, if you have chosen the market well, you can allow it to do all the heavy lifting in terms of value creation: over a 10- or 20-year period, the property will date, and the market will grow due to population growth, income growth, investments in infrastructure and so on.

Contrary to popular opinion, I think it is fine to pay a little more for a property you want because you are the only person who fully understands the value that you are getting.

How to not f*ck it up

The best way to think like a local and not f*ck it up is to take your time. Learn about a market, spend time in the streets, see open homes, review previous sales and build confidence in your knowledge. You will never have perfect knowledge and all the information you want but, with enough time, you will develop a good understanding of the things you need to know and will feel more confident in your decision-making.

As they say, 'Haste makes waste'. Never get sucked into the heat of a market or any one property in particular. Yes, by taking your time you may miss out on some properties, but you can rest assured that there will always be something else for you to buy. Remember, all the money is made when you buy, so take the time you need to feel confident and get a deal done.

On the other hand, do not sit on your hands for too long. I think it is important that, once you have a clear understanding of what you want and have the budget to buy it, you go out there and get it. I have met a lot of could-have, should-have, would-have people that just never did. They spent too much time watching the market and, after a year or more, didn't act. Overanalysing and avoiding the inevitable leap of faith is a great way to f*ck things up. The beauty of buying property is that time will heal almost all wounds.

For all your preliminary research into the market, you can use many of the websites I've already mentioned (which are also listed at the back of this book), but another one to add to your repertoire is walkscore.com. This is a great website for getting a sense of how walkable a suburb is and what's nearby.

Chapter 7

Understand Different Properties – New Versus Existing Property

After you have chosen the market (or markets) that you like the most, it's time to choose a property. There is a lot to cover when it comes to understanding different properties, so I've split this information over two chapters: in this chapter I break down the pros, cons and things to think about when buying new or existing property, and in the next chapter I dive into the details of each property type (apartments, townhouses and houses).

New property

In recent years, new and off-the-plan properties have deservedly built a bad reputation. This is due to the bad workmanship and terrible delivery of many projects across Australia. During the property boom of 2018, Australians were developing about 200,000 properties a year – 50,000 above the average. This boom in construction was influenced by an influx of foreign investors, particularly from China, looking to buy brand new property in Australia due to the laws and tax structures around investment, which were written in such a way that these investors were limited to buying new real estate.

This strong demand was great for the industry because it meant that there were ready buyers for almost all new developments that entered the market. However, many new and inexperienced developers, builders, tradespeople, planners, certifiers and engineers entered the market, and a few short years later their properties were showing major issues. This is when horror stories about defective apartment developments emerged, with buildings cracking, sinking, flooding and becoming unliveable.

It is important to note that this is not an industry-wide issue. Yes, there are some new builds that are not delivered to a high standard, but it is important not to allow the minority of new developments to ruin your perception of the majority. Residential construction has been one of the economic pillars of Australia's development as a country. All these old buildings you see around were once new, and the price you would pay for property in those buildings today is far higher than what the properties originally sold for.

In this section I take you through some of the pros and cons of buying new property, along with some tips on how to buy a new property and avoid many of the issues and problems that you have heard about.

The pros of buying brand new property

There are a number of often-overlooked benefits of buying brand new property. It is beneficial to have a broad understanding of these potential benefits since you may find that, despite what your friends and family think, this type of property may suit your lifestyle or investment needs best.

People usually prefer new cars, phones, computers and clothes because, with each iteration, the product gets better. The same is true with property. New properties are great because they are made from the latest building technologies, materials and designs. This is good for energy efficiency, sound and heat insulation, airflow and natural light. Despite some people's perceptions, building standards have improved over time and it has become harder to develop property due to the high standards that buildings must meet. Standards differ between different states and territories, but properties need to meet certain requirements regarding lighting, ventilation, energy efficiency and acoustics before they are approved and can be delivered. New materials help builders to meet these standards and, depending on the property, they may also far surpass the standards. This makes living in these properties a real comfort.

Many new properties have been designed for modern living. They have plenty of storage, home offices, open living spaces, good security and up-to-date technology. After you have lived in a new property with quality appliances, hardware and smart design, it can be jarring to move back into something older.

Because people like to live in new properties, they will pay a premium to enjoy all their conveniences. If you rent out a new property, you will generally get more rent than for a similar property that is older. Also, you will have a wider choice of applicants and can therefore be more selective about who will tenant the property. In a tight rental market, you can raise the rents, and when the market is slower you have room to lower rents to quickly secure a tenant. This means that new properties are usually vacant for less time and make for reliable rental properties.

If you've bought a good new property, you will generally receive few calls from your rental manager, roommate or partner about repairs and maintenance. If things break within the first few years, they are likely to be covered by warranties or may fit within the builders' defects liability period. For people who want a stress-free property with little intervention, new properties' repairs are generally very minimal for the first five years (and up to ten years with good properties). As an investor, it is great to have your property running properly, earning you an income and growing in value all in the background while you are out living your life.

Australia has a tax system that encourages you to invest and allows you to claim expenses as deductions against your investments to reduce your tax bill. For real estate, this means you can claim expenses such as management fees, water and council rates and the interest on your mortgage. You can also claim for depreciation of the building and the fixtures and fittings in the property as your new property gets older and experiences wear and tear. The building is calculated at 2.5 per cent per year for 40 years; the fixtures and fittings – such as your lights, carpet, floorboards, oven and shower – all have different depreciable lives. This can get you thousands of dollars back at the end of each financial year. There are whole books written on this, with lots of rules about how it works, but I do not want to bore you with the details here; if you want to know more, take a look at my Wealthi Academy on YouTube (youtube.com/@Wealthi) or my website (wealthi.com.au/academy). You can also talk to your accountant.

The state, territory and federal governments run a number of different initiatives and policies to help people get into the property market. Historically they have incentivised people to buy newly built homes and off-the-plan properties because this promotes new construction, creating supply and new jobs. It is worth looking at what government incentives are available because, depending on the price you are paying, your income and the state or territory that you intend on buying property in, they can be pretty generous when it comes to new builds, particularly for your first home.

Some people buy new properties simply because it gives them access to a building, location or vista where there are no existing properties. The launch of a new land estate or building can be very exciting because it offers something rare, unique or simply great quality. Getting access to these new properties can be great from a lifestyle perspective but can also make for excellent investment opportunities. In new estates you can take your pick of properties with the right land size, orientation and distance from the retail hub, park, school and other amenities. Buying into a new building in a lucrative location can also make for a great investment if the property is one of very few and delivered by a brand-name architect or designer; these properties carry strong demand.

Not all brand new property for sale is completed and ready to rent out or move into: you can also buy brand new property off the plan. As the name suggests, this involves buying a property based on a set of plans, computer-generated images and developer-provided information. Buying off-the-plan property comes with the benefit that it takes some time to build and complete after purchase, which can allow you to pay a deposit to secure the property and then have some time to save up a bigger deposit while it is completed. With most off-the-plan properties, you are required to pay a 10 per cent deposit to exchange on the contract and secure the property. While it is being built, you are not required to pay any more than that and only need to start paying the remaining 90 per cent of your money at the end of construction, once your property is complete. This is when you need to get your loan from the bank and start to pay it back.

What this means for some investors is that they can use this time to their advantage by using market movements to make money on the growth of the asset while it is under construction. I did this with my second Newcastle property. I paid a 5 per cent deposit on a two-bedroom apartment worth $460,000. It cost me $23,000 to exchange on the contracts to secure the property, and it took a little over 18 months for construction to be completed. Over this 18-month period I knew that some investments were going to be made in the city of Newcastle that would drive up the value of property in the market. Also, during this extra time, I saved more money for a deposit so I would have enough to get a loan and settle the property upon completion. When this property was completed, it was valued at $580,000, which meant that I had made $120,000 over that 18-month period. This was more than I would have been able to save over five years if I ate nothing but baked beans. Needless to say, I was very happy, since this gave me the boost I needed to buy my next property. (Note that while the timing of the property's completion can be used to your advantage, it can also come with disadvantages, which I will cover in the cons section.)

The cons of buying brand new property

One obvious downside of buying brand new property is that new things cost more than old things, so buying a new property costs more than buying an old property of similar size, amenity and location. This means that you are using more of your money to enter the property market, which, depending on your financial means, could be the difference between buying one or multiple properties.

New properties cost more because they generally have every-thing that you need in them (appropriate for the area). They are fully specced and have all the bells and whistles, which means there is little to no room for further improvements. Some people like to buy older properties so they can renovate, add value and use the growth in the asset for their next investment. Though you can make some improve-ments to new properties, opportunities are very limited and would normally lead you to overcapitalise on the asset, which is when you spend more money upgrading a property than you gain in value from the upgrade. An example of this would be spending $100,000 on a detailed water feature for a property worth $500,000: it is unlikely that the water feature would add $100,000 in value to the property.

Buying off the plan in a rising market can allow you to make a profit on your deposit while it is under construction, but the opposite is also true if the market falls or you receive a negative valuation on the property. It is not uncommon to buy a property off the plan for a price that is higher than the property's value at completion, which means you need to put in more money to secure the loan. Here is an example: you buy a $500,000 property and, when it is completed two years later, your bank orders a valuation that comes back at $450,000. This means that, in order for you to get the loan, you need to pay the $50,000 difference between the valuation and the contract price. This means that your property has a lower loan amount, which is good, but it also means that it has taken more of your cash to take ownership of the property. This is an expensive example, but I have heard of much worse situations than this, so it is very important to be careful with this type of investment and build up a solid cash buffer to reduce your risk.

How to not f*ck it up

When buying a brand new or off-the-plan property, there are a few things to consider in order to reduce your risk, protect your investment and not f*ck it up.

After you have chosen your location, make a list of the brand new developments that are available for sale. Next, take a closer look at each site and see which one suits your needs best. To do this, de-risk and qualify each of development using the criteria in this section.

Developers do not need to have their development approved by the local authority to start selling, so the first criterion you need to check is whether the development has been approved and, if not, when it is likely to be approved. This is vitally important because it tells you whether there is a risk that you might not get the property you were promised. You might be putting a deposit down on a property that won't get approved, or perhaps it will get approved but with conditions that affect your property, or it will just take longer than expected. Local councils, the city and even the state or territory government can be involved in the process, and it can take years for the approval to come in. After all of this, the property then still needs to be built, which takes even more time. If you are going to buy a property that has not been approved, it is important for you to weigh the risk against the reward; in some cases, it may suit your strategy because you are buying at a great price and are in no rush for the property to be completed.

When buying a property off the plan, it might seem strange to do so but you are well within your rights to ask the agent or developer whether the new project is fully funded and ready to start construction. Property developers and builders often need to finance the developments they intend on delivering; some rare companies can afford to cash-fund the purchase of the land, plans, marketing and build, but most cannot. These companies will use banks, and banks typically have a bunch of conditions that need to be satisfied before they will release money to a developer. It is risky buying a property off the plan prior to the development getting funding. One condition of funding from the bank may be for the developer to pre-sell a certain number of properties, and there is no guarantee that the developer will reach this target, so you may be stuck with your deposit sitting in a trust account for years with the delivery of the property in doubt. However, though risky, there are also rewards that come from buying at this early stage. Since the developer likely needs to get these pre-sales to secure funding, this puts you in a position to negotiate for discounts, different commercial terms and upgrades to the property.

They say, 'Timing is everything', and this is not far from the truth. Timing is a very important criteria to assess before committing to buying a property off the plan. It is very easy for an agent or sales representative to just give you some timelines, but the more you know, the better you'll be able to verify their accuracy. In addition to approval and finance, here are the important milestones to understand in a development:

- *Building commencement:* As with all stages of a development timeline, building commencement can be delayed due to planning, finance and sales requirements. If there is certainty around when construction will start, you can then figure out when it is likely to be completed.

- *Construction program:* All developments have a building program and, after construction has started, there will be more certainty around completion, so learning about the program is important. It is common for the building program to run late, so it helps to budget a few extra months into whatever is being quoted.

- *Completion:* Once you are pretty clear on when the property will be completed, you can get ready. This means coordinating your finances and insurances and, if you are planning to rent the property out, getting a property manager ready.

The big risk with buying a brand new property, especially if it is off the plan, is the success of its delivery. All these questions about quality, approvals, finance and timing come back to who is delivering the property. When you decide to sign a contract and commit to buying a property, you are effectively going into business with the developer and their partners. You are trusting that they have all the skills, knowledge and experience to complete the project and give you the promised property at completion. So, before committing to a property, it is important to understand who you are going into business with and learn if they have the capacity to deliver on their promises. There are many businesses and consultants involved in delivering a development, but the three main parties who hold the most influence are the following:

- *The developer:* This is the dealmaker who brings everything together and is ultimately responsible for the success or failure of the project. The developer is the person who controls the land, secures the approval and finance, coordinates the sales and marketing and then appoints the builder to finish it all off. They pay all the bills and make the profit or loss at the end of the project.

- *The builder:* The builder can sometimes be the developer but not always. They are contracted to create the construction program, and then project-manage and deliver the development.

- *The architect:* The architect is the visionary who imagines the building, drafts the plans and creates the construction drawings for the builder. They design the building and are responsible for how it all feels when it is completed. As happens with great artists, some people follow specific architects to buy the properties that they design.

After you have noted who is involved in delivering the development, it is important to take a close look at each business and assess them as best you can against the following criteria:

- *Experience:* The bigger the project, the more complex it is likely to be and the more important experience becomes. Some of the best ways to determine experience are to find out how long each business has been operating and to look at their previous projects. All good businesses will proudly advertise their past projects, and today it is easy to simply look up Google and Trustpilot reviews.

However, always remember that the best research you can do for real estate is away from the computer: after you have checked the reviews, go for a drive and see in person how these past projects have aged. This will be very telling of their work and give you all the insight you need into the property you are considering.

- *Expertise:* When looking at the experience of each business and their body of work, there is value in looking closely at what specifically they have worked on. This can be very helpful in avoiding businesses with lots of experience but not in the type of project that your property is part of. This has the potential to save you lots of time, heartache and money.

- *Earnings:* This is a hard criterion to determine because you really do not know what happens behind closed doors, and sometimes even the biggest businesses have cash issues. For about $60 you can run a credit check on a company at equifax.com.au and learn about the business and its directors. This report will tell you any adverse information about other companies the directors are involved with or closed and their invoice payment history, which is a quick way to see if there are any red flags. However, dodgy businesses can hide these issues. The only other way to determine this, particularly for the builder and developer, is to ask about current jobs that they are working on and completing. These businesses make most of their money at the end of projects, so it is a good sign if they have sites they are completing.

You will never have 100 per cent transparency and all the information. This is where the risk–reward balance comes into play. When doing your risk assessment and determining whether you want to buy one property over another, remember that everything comes at a cost. The cost of buying from a well-known business and brand is the premium price you pay for the property, whereas the cost of going for a cheaper property from a smaller developer and builder is the uncertainty and potential problems you may have in the future.

However, when doing your assessment, don't put too much value in the brand or company. Companies are made up of people, and it is the people who deliver the property. You may be dealing with a new business run by experienced people; in this instance you have the benefit of a cheaper price due to the company being new and a great product because it is being delivered by great people.

The big tip with buying brand new or off-the-plan properties is to always ask lots of questions, do your due diligence and look past the pretty brochures. Then, after you have done your computer work, get outside and see property before buying.

Existing property

Existing properties are what most people buy. This is the real estate that you can touch and feel, that is traded on and off market after it has been completed. There are a number of pros and cons to buying existing property.

The pros of buying existing property

One of the things that I love the most about buying real estate is getting out there and experiencing it. I enjoy the whole process of driving to the place, walking down the street, taking in all the sights and walking through the property. Within minutes you get a sense of the property and pick up details that Google Maps and photos did not show you. There is a lot to experience when you go out and see a property that you can easily miss when you are simply shopping from your phone or computer. In many cases the old saying 'the photos don't do it justice' is very true for both good and bad; there are some excellent photographers out there who can suggest more than what might be there but, in some cases, a view, an outlook, natural light or a breeze cannot be caught by the camera and simply needs to be experienced.

While walking down the street you might notice that there are huge power lines overhead. In the property, perhaps rooms feel a little tighter than the plans suggest, or maybe the property is much closer to the loud train station than you expected. There might be hundreds of other details that you simply would not have noticed without going and seeing the property for yourself. Being able to go and inspect a property is extremely valuable, especially when buying your own home. This is as much an emotional journey as an investment one, and your gut will tell you more in minutes then your mind will over many nights of research.

When buying an investment property, inspecting it in person is valuable, but some people feel very comfortable simply doing all the research and maths from the comfort of their home. They do all their homework, engage a solicitor, get their finance and buy the property without ever seeing it. This is more common than you might think, and it can work very well. This method helps to keep emotions out of the investment decision.

The beauty of buying real estate is that it is tangible, and so most of what you need to know to make a good investment decision can be examined, researched or paid for. You will never have all the facts but, when buying an existing property, you can at least inspect it and get reports from professionals to find out most of what you need to know. Some properties you inspect will be old enough that any big problems would be easily noticeable, but young enough that it will be many years before serious wear and tear degrades the building, appliances, fixtures and fittings. Big problems will be immediately obvious to a trained eye after a quick run through the property. If you don't have a tradesperson in the family, it is easy and cheap enough to order the required reports to find out what issues the property has and is likely to incur over time. These reports are extremely helpful, since they tell you exactly what you are getting and, if there are problems, you can at least budget for them. However, I must note that even if you've inspected the property and got all the reports done, there is still a chance that you won't catch every issue.

As mentioned in the section on new property, older things generally cost less than newer things. If you are happy to forgo the comforts of newer properties, you can save some money, which is very handy if you are just starting out or wanting to get into markets that would otherwise be out of reach. If you are really game and can tolerate a house that is in desperate need of repairs or has a terrible layout, you can really steal a bargain. The truth is that most people like to avoid the issues and pain that come with buying something old. Problems mean that you need to invest time and money. Typically, the more issues there are with a property, the cheaper it will be.

I was able to buy my holiday house in Nelson Bay (discussed in chapter 1) for a steal. The property was a three-bedroom house on stilts with all original 1950s kitchen, bathroom and carpet. There was a lot of work that needed to be done, but it was on a big block, had good bones and boasted a beautiful view out to the mountains and water. Charlotte and I bought it for $660,000 when homes with smaller blocks on the same street were selling for $100,000 to $300,000 more. We were able to pick up a steal that would later become a great investment.

There's a great saying that illustrates the value you can create in buying old properties and fixing them up: 'You get paid proportionally to the problems that you fix'. There are many homeowners and investors who have made millions of dollars by buying properties with potential, renovating them and selling them for a profit. There is more involved than what I have described here, but it can be very profitable.

People are happy to pay a premium for other people to do the work for them. Property is a big investment, and it takes a lot of time, creativity and money to renovate homes, hence the profit that you can make if you do it correctly. The benefit of running this process on your own home is that you do not need to pay capital gains tax on the profit you have made; you can use the uplift in value to pull the equity out as a loan from the bank without needing to sell the property and pay taxes. It all starts with creating value.

The cons of buying existing property

There is a wide range of existing property available, from homes that are barely a year old to homes that have been around since before Australia's federation. This means there is a wide margin of error when generalising about existing property; so, in this section, I highlight some of the more extreme examples to be mindful of.

One of the risks with buying existing real estate is that, even if you have had all the professional reports done, you may still uncover unexpected issues. Generally, the older the property, the more likely you are to encounter nasty surprises, either during renovation or over time as things degrade or break. If you don't have a budget for wear and tear, this can make your life very difficult.

My fiancée and I bought an old home in the west of Sydney and were looking to do a major renovation. We were redoing the kitchen and bathroom and knocking down walls. We had a tight budget and were looking to renovate in a pretty thrifty manner. However, when we decided to redo one of the bathrooms on the first storey of the house, we got a surprise: we were doing some demolition work and, as we removed the old floor tiles, parts of the rotting floor were coming up with each tile, creating a hole that grew with each tile we removed. It turned out that the previous owner had either done no waterproofing or a poor job of it, and all the wood had rotted and was just being held together by the old tiles and grout. This meant that we had to pull out all the flooring on the first floor and completely redo the second bathroom as well as the laundry. Needless to say, this was not an expense that we had anticipated, and so our small budget had to grow.

Renovating an old home will take more time than you think, cost more money than you anticipate and teach you plenty of hard lessons. Even the best in the business – construction companies that build homes every day – encounter issues regularly, so there are plenty of pitfalls that amateurs can get stuck in. The critical thing is to recognise this when going into a project and prepare yourself for the worst. Optimism will get you started but pessimism will keep you prepared.

How to not f*ck it up

The key to avoid f*cking up buying property in the existing market is to go in with your eyes and ears wide open and not skimp on the things that matter. It can seem like an unnecessary expense to pay hundreds of dollars for professionals to examine your property and write up reports, especially if you need to order these reports for more than one property, but they can save you thousands – potentially hundreds of thousands – of dollars. Here are the reports you should consider buying before investing in real estate:

· *Building inspection report:* A building inspection report includes a summary of the inspector's findings and a list of any major and minor defects, as well as suggested solutions. It should also include photographs for you to reference. This report will give you a clear picture of the state of the property so you can make an informed decision about whether you want to buy the property.

- *Pest inspection report:* A pest inspection report helps you identify activity or damage caused by pests such as termites, borers and wood rot (fungi). This is separate from the building report but also important since it highlights issues that are easy to miss unless a professional has made an inspection.

- *Strata report:* A strata report should provide precise details of what is happening within a building or complex. It helps you understand the history of the building and normally covers items such as who the current owner is; the quarterly levies for the property; the voting rights and unit entitlement; whether or not there are any current or proposed special levies (additional contributions outside your quarterly levies that may be raised for building defects or major works); whether or not the strata scheme complies with fire requirements, work health and safety obligations and asbestos management; how much is in the capital works or sinking fund and the administrative fund, and if any of the funds are in deficit; if there are any current legal matters; and much more.

Chapter 8

Understand Different Properties – Property Types

When buying real estate, everyone has an opinion (and normally a strong one). They will be quick to tell you what they think is the right way, the wrong way and the absolute worst way. Alongside the battle in philosophy between brand new and existing property (covered in chapter 7) is the battle between the property types. There are those who swear by buying property with land only, and there are those who would never want the headache of a house and swear by apartments.

The truth is that all property types can make for good or bad investments, but it comes down to what you are trying to achieve. An apple isn't better than an avocado, but it is if you are making apple pie. In this chapter, I cover each of the property types and some of the pros and cons of each, as well as what each property type is most suitable for.

Apartments

Apartments make for great investments and secure, convenient homes. As a general rule they do not typically grow in value as much as houses, but they do have higher rental yields, and they make for great entry points into markets that would otherwise be inaccessible. Apartments offer many advantages that you simply do not get from houses. Later in life they make for good homes to downsize to, offering security and conveniences that would be much too expensive to have in a house.

The pros of buying an apartment

The first major advantage apartments have over other property types is in **price**. Apartments make for good entry-level real estate. Since they are smaller and can be developed in larger, scalable numbers, they are cheaper than houses in the same location. They are good for first-time buyers and investors because they require less money to buy than houses and allow access to locations and lifestyles that would otherwise be out of reach. The cheaper price means that homeowners and investors can enter the market earlier and use the investment to leverage into bigger homes or investments later. It also allows them to stay in locations where they feel comfortable buying and gives them time to learn about property, become more comfortable and keep on growing.

Many people like apartments for the **security** they offer. A lot of old developments and almost all new developments have security front doors, single front door access and drive-in garages with buzzer or fob entry; and many apartments exist above the ground floor, adding another layer of security. For people who live on their own, are less able or getting older, this security is a huge advantage over what houses can offer. Many people would not even consider a house because the multiple ground-floor entry points make them feel exposed.

Apartments also deliver **convenience**, given that they are usually located at the centre of metropolitan hubs and city fringes, close to amenities. This is due to state and local council land zoning. Governments like to have high-density residential zoning around transport and suburb centres since it brings greater commercial activity and delivers services to the greatest number of people. As well as the convenience of location, some apartment buildings also offer convenience through a huge number of amenities – especially in the newer developments – such as pools, gyms, games rooms, dog wash bays, co-working spaces and spas. This type of convenience is very attractive to homeowners and renters – and, therefore, investors. People who choose apartments for the conveniences are less likely to need a car due to the property's proximity to services and amenities. Furthermore, they are able to save on the cost of subscriptions to many of the amenities their building offers.

Apartments typically have a higher rent-to-price ratio (**yield**) than houses. This is attractive to investors since it means they can get strong cash flow from the property, making it easier to hold the property over the long term. They may even be making money from the property via positive cash flow, or at least making significant progress paying off their ownership costs.

Apartments in good strata buildings and complexes make for good homes and great passive investments because a significant portion of the **maintenance** is handled for you. Some of these developments have committees, building managers, strata managers, cleaners and even gardeners and utilities teams. Others are not big enough to warrant all these people and expenses but are nonetheless very well run. The people involved in running the building take on the stress and work needed to keep the properties well maintained and upgraded when necessary. So, for someone who does not want the bother of mowing lawns and doing upkeep and maintenance on a property, apartments make for a great purchase.

The cons of buying an apartment

Apartments are strata titled, which means they are a part of a strata scheme and make up a piece of a larger complex. Everything in the apartment is 100 per cent yours to use and maintain, but the common areas – such as the hallways, lifts, gardens, pool and rooftop – are all shared with the other strata owners. Since you share these spaces, you need to share in the cost of maintenance, insurances, services and upgrades. These **fees** vary between states and territories and from one development to another, and they can become quite expensive over time. Well-run buildings without issues are generally OK and their strata fees don't normally increase too much. However, if you buy into a poorly run strata with a bad building, things can become problematic and expensive. For issues that pop up out of the blue, the strata committee can raise special levies, and if there are continual issues that cost a lot to maintain they can also just increase the strata fee.

Different developments have different **rules and regulations**: some can be very relaxed, while others can be extremely uptight and prohibitive about what is allowed in the building and what is not. For instance, some buildings will not allow you to short-term-lease your property, or they will have restrictions on the size and number of animals you can have in your apartment. For some people this is not an issue because the rules create order and a nice place to live, but for others these rules can be quite prohibitive to the way they want to live or run their investment.

Not everyone likes their **neighbours**, and in apartment buildings you have quite a few. For some people, sharing multiple walls, floor and ceiling with other people can feel restrictive. Depending on the building you have bought in, you can share common spaces with all sorts of people and their problems. In most cases there are no issues, but those people who are unlucky to have bad neighbours or who are particularly sensitive to noise may be less happy in apartments. I used to live next door to two drag queens, and every Friday and Saturday night I could hear their high heels running up and down the stairs as they got ready to go out. At that point in time, I was a young man living with my girlfriend; we had parties and were friendly with our neighbours, so this didn't bother us. I am now engaged and have a baby, so those high heels would now drive me insane.

Historically, apartments have achieved **slower growth** in value than houses. This is, of course, a generalisation – some apartments grow much faster than some houses – but on average you should be prepared to experience slower growth for an apartment than a house in the same market. According to CoreLogic data, Australian house values increased 453 per cent in the 30 years prior to 2022, compared to 307 per cent across Australian units. The 30-year annualised growth for houses was 5.6 per cent and for units was 4.7 per cent.

Townhouses

Townhouses are normally smaller than houses internally and externally but bigger than units. They have a bit of a backyard and may share some walls, but not always. They are sometimes referred to as the 'missing middle', since they occupy that space between houses and apartments from a size and price perspective. They tend to polarise investors and homeowners – depending on who you talk to, people either love them or hate them and say they are the best or worst of houses and apartments. Personally, I think Australia needs more of them; they provide an option for people to step up into from apartments or down into from houses.

The pros of buying a townhouse

Townhouses deliver **affordability**. Relative to houses in the same area, townhouses give people much of what they want from a house but without the price tag. Most will either have a front yard or backyard with a bit of grass. Since townhouses are normally compact, they can be split over two levels, which gives people the space they wouldn't get in an apartment. Townhouses make for great homes and investments because they allow purchasers to get into markets that would otherwise be out of reach; the fact that they take up less space means they cost less than nearby houses.

Townhouses also deliver **convenience**. Councils zone land in the inner cities and around train stations as high density, and the zoning gets gradually lower in density as you move away from these areas. This means that these compact homes are commonly built close to public transport, amenities in city centres and on the city fringes, allowing purchasers to get close to the action.

Townhouses, like apartments, are generally part of a strata scheme. This means that there is a committee and managers to handle the **maintenance** of common property and organise insurances. As noted previously, this is great when you have a functional owners' corporation or body corporate and a good development, but not if you don't. Further to this, since townhouses are compact, there is less to maintain than with houses. There may be a small bit of grass for a backyard but, other than this and the living spaces, there isn't much that needs to be maintained outside your property that strata doesn't look after.

The cons of buying a townhouse

One issue townhouses can have is **size**. While bigger than apartments, townhouses are still generally smaller than houses. They are generally designed to fit on a small block of land and therefore have a compact internal design. Townhouses are also usually built in clusters, which means they are all quite close together and in some instances also share walls. This can make some townhouses feel poky and confining if you are after lots of open space and privacy.

As with apartments, townhouses generally fit within a strata scheme and are therefore governed by plenty of **rules and regulations**. As mentioned, this can be good when done well, since it allows for the estate and community facilities to be well looked after. It is also common for strata to create covenants and enforce rules that require owners to take care of the townhouses in a certain manner. This can be good as it requires neighbours to upkeep their homes, but it can also become restrictive for people who want to do as they please with their property. If you want the freedom to paint your garage door red or make lots of alterations to your property, townhouses in a strata scheme may not be for you.

Though they are affordable and tend to have strong rental returns, townhouses are closer to apartments than houses when it comes to their **resale value**, which means they tend to grow in value more slowly.

Houses

The good old house on a quarter-acre block is the great Australian dream. Many locals and migrants aspire to eventually own a piece of dirt with a house on it so they can raise their family and start paying off their 30-year loan with the bank. They want some space where their families can grow and a bit of grass for the kids to play on. Houses hold a special place in many people's hearts, and it is this romance that has driven the price of houses to grow by 453.1 per cent – or $760,879 – over the 30 years up to 2022. Unfortunately, for many people looking to buy their first home or investment, this huge growth has meant that they cannot afford to buy a house. Fortunately, not all houses have grown faster than units and, for those after more space in their home, there are creative solutions out there – such as rentvesting, which I cover in chapter 11.

The pros of buying a house

Houses in major metropolitan areas have experienced the best **price growth** of any property type over the past 30 years, and this is likely to continue for the foreseeable future. People really value the space, privacy and flexibility that comes from owning a plot of land with a house on it. As the populations of cities continue to grow, house values go upwards, with developers usually knocking down houses to build units. Cities also grow outwards; this is called urban sprawl and, as this happens, the houses that are closest to the city, beaches and amenities continue to grow in price. If you are an investor who is looking for strong price growth above all else, you are most likely to get this growth by buying a house. However, buyer beware: not all houses are equal, so you still need to be careful.

Houses are great to buy for **space**. They accommodate more bedrooms, bigger kitchens, multiple living areas and outdoor space. In a post-COVID-19 world, space has become more valuable than ever. We were stuck in our homes for months at a time and this caused people to think about what they need from a home much more carefully. The option to work from home is available to more people and this has increased the value of extra space. The extra room could be an office, a gym, a future baby room or a sanctuary. Space has always been a valuable feature in a property and houses are the bigger form of real estate.

Owning a house with land gives you more **flexibility** than an apartment or townhouse. As long as you comply with the rules of your local council, you can make alterations and upgrades and develop the property to your liking and advantage. With a house you can landscape the backyard, add a pool, add a level, renovate the entire building or demolish it and subdivide the block. Houses give you a great deal of flexibility to do as you please with your property without the rules and regulations that come with being in a strata property.

This can be hugely beneficial whether the house is your own home or an investment property. It is common for people to live in a house for decades and, over that time, make all the little improvements that make the house home. On the other end of the spectrum, people use houses as successful investment vehicles to add value through building and development. This flexibility is one of the biggest advantages this property type has over the others.

Many people really value the **privacy** that you get when living in a house. You may have a handful of neighbours, and some might be able to look into your backyard, but houses usually offer more privacy than townhouses and apartments. Houses do not share walls or require you to share facilities with others. Many houses have large setbacks from the street, some are elevated with views and others are in secluded areas with very few neighbours. People who value privacy are generally willing to pay a premium for this luxury, which can be hard to come by with the other property types.

The cons of buying a house

A major issue when it comes to buying a house is **affordability**. Over the last 30 years houses in major metropolitan hubs have grown in value at a tremendous rate, making them unaffordable for most of the market, especially new property owners. The most desirable properties achieve the fastest growth but come at a cost, and this can put buyers in compromising financial situations. The pressure to buy a house and acquire nearly insurmountable levels of debt can put a lot of stress on a family and cause undue hardship. This type of pressure is usually what causes people to make mistakes, overreach and get caught out. When the pressure is too much and a family cannot meet its payment obligations, they are then forced to sell, and this is how people lose money in real estate.

Houses come with more space, front yards and backyards, sometimes pools, and more moving parts. This makes **maintenance** harder and more expensive. If it is your own home, you'll notice how much goes into looking after a house compared to a unit or townhouse. When the house is an investment, you'll need to make allowances for upkeep and make sure you have a good property manager to keep your tenants in line. Little issues that are left unattended can become much bigger issues down the road, so it makes good sense to stay on top of maintenance and any issues that pop up with your property.

Historically, houses receive less rent than units and townhouses proportional to the price you pay to buy them. This is a generalisation, of course, and the difference can vary between locations, but this typically makes houses more expensive to run year on year. A lower **yield** means you earn less income in rent than with other properties and can mean that the investment costs you money to run each year. This is OK if it fits within your budget and strategy but can be very frustrating if the property is not growing in value and is also putting pressure on your household.

How to not f*ck it up

The beautiful thing about investing in real estate is that it is really pretty simple. A lot of what you need to learn can be read about, listened to through podcasts and seen on YouTube, but most is learnt from experience. You are buying a real, tangible asset that you experience every day. Your experiences with real estate at home, visiting friends and family and doing open house inspections teaches you about each investment class, and you'll pick up a lot of useful information by asking a few questions along the way. Much of what you have read in this chapter is not rocket science and becomes familiar knowledge as you are exposed to real estate over the years.

Buying your own home is a very personal experience, and much of your criteria is determined first by budget and then by how you like to live. These personal circumstances will likely determine the type of property you end up buying. For instance, when I was in the early stages of my career and my relationship with Charlotte, we wanted a fun place to live: to be close to the action with some greenery nearby, and to have new appliances. With my budget and criteria set, we ended up in a two-bedroom apartment in St Peters, Sydney. These were fun years: we entertained often, were close to Newtown and had easy access to the city and Sydney Park. At the time of writing this book, we have a baby, and our budget and criteria have dramatically changed. With a growing family, we want to be away from the action: to have space, walking access to nature and some peace and quiet. Before, a new apartment suited me to a tee, whereas now I would much prefer a larger house.

If you are buying an investment property, your criteria are determined by your budget, risk tolerance, goals and strategy. This should be a much less emotional decision that is largely governed by logic, maths and good sense. The type of property does not matter so long as it fits within your strategy.

Remember one thing: you will almost never get everything that you want out of the property. If it is perfect, it is likely to be too expensive; if it is affordable, there are likely to be some issues. Pick a property that hits your key criteria and give yourself some wiggle room on the other criteria so you can make the purchase work.

Chapter 9

Pick Your Property

Here comes the good bit but easily the most nerve-wrenching: picking a property. A whole book could be written on this alone, but I will try and distil how to pick your property into two key elements:

1. Goal: what am I trying to achieve by buying this property?
2. Attributes: what are the specifications that matter to me to achieve my goal?

Goal

Your goal is very important. This is your north star and keeps you out of trouble when things get a little confusing or murky. After all, it is common that where you start your property journey isn't where you will end it. You will learn a lot about what you like and dislike, along with your must-haves and absolutely-nots. The power of a good goal is that it keeps you focused. After you have seen a ton of property and spoken to a bunch of people, you may find yourself getting confused; the goal brings you back to what is important.

So, before you do anything, you need to get clear on your goal and what you want to achieve through buying a property. Set out your criteria and understand your must-haves, want-to-haves, budget and time frame. It is helpful to break down your goal into the key attributes that you are looking for, and then score and rank each attribute from most to least important. You'll find that getting out and experiencing these attributes will bring you clarity and put your criteria into perspective.

Case study: the goal and key criteria for our Nelson Bay property

Here is an example of the goal and key criteria Charlotte and I had for our most recent purchase (at the time of writing).

Goal

Buy an inexpensive holiday house so that we can escape the hustle and bustle of Sydney on a Thursday or Friday night and come back for work on Monday.

Must-haves

Budget: Less than $700,000

Distance: Max 3 hours from Sydney

Location: Walking distance from the water and town
            centre – so, about 1 km

Property: Freestanding house with good bones that we can
            add value to

Want-to-haves

· Northern aspect with good ventilation and natural light
· An outlook over the trees and ideally some view of the water
· Good privacy with few neighbours looking into the property.

The budget, distance and location helped to narrow down my search a lot and focused my attention on a few key areas. Since this was just a holiday house, we learnt that we did not want to spend too much, and the urge to visit on weekends meant that we did not want to travel more than three hours.

Our property criteria were pretty loose. We were happy to do extensive work to the house we ended up buying if it meant that the house could be closer to town and the water. If we ranked having a nicer, more liveable home more highly, this would have required us to loosen our criteria on either the location or the budget. My family and I love to walk everywhere, and I have really learnt to enjoy the process of designing and building homes, and we had budgeted enough cash to do this.

This may seem like a pretty simple exercise but it does take time for you to narrow it down and get clarity on all factors. Charlotte and I went on many road trips and visited a lot of open homes. We spent quite a bit of time in front of the spreadsheet really thinking about how much money we were prepared to spend and what we wanted from this property.

How to not f*ck it up

The big learning from this chapter is to write out your goal and then set your key criteria. From here, test out your criteria by getting out there and experiencing as much of what you want as possible. The key here is to not be too rigid with your criteria in the pursuit of achieving your goal. Getting out there, working on your budget and learning about what you want will help you rank and establish what really matters to you, and this will help you home in on what you are trying to achieve.

Attributes

When picking your property, you will no doubt be looking for a number of key attributes to satisfy your needs. Depending on your goals, you will need to keep an eye out for different property attributes, both physical and on paper. If you are looking for a property to make your home, it is likely you will be looking for features such as a lot of natural light or proximity to schools and transport. Most of the attributes needed to meet the criteria will be tangible and physical in nature. If the property is being bought for investment purposes, then it is likely you will be looking for attributes that look great on paper, such as rental yields, growth rates, vacancy rates and tax incentives. In this section I take you through some of the key attributes to keep an eye out for that will improve your quality of living in a home and improve the nature of your investment.

Physical attributes

Physical attributes are the qualities of the property that you can see, touch, feel and experience. Many of these attributes affect you day to day and impact how you feel about the property. When you eventually choose to sell or lease your property, you will get more money if the property stirs a positive emotional response. Decisions made through emotion can often cause people to pay more than if they were to make the decision purely through logic.

Each of the following physical attributes may rank higher or lower on your list depending on what you want out of a property, but there are some attributes that most people value and that will make for a much nicer property. These are often the attributes that make the property stand out from the rest. Many of these have also been noted in previous chapters, but I elaborate on each attribute in more detail here.

Like plants, people love light – lots of light! Having the right aspect determines how much **sunlight** gets into the property, and having the right features and design ensures you feel it. Finishes such as floor-to-ceiling glass, light wells and living areas facing in the right direction all impact how much light gets into the property and your experience with it. A bright property that is flooded with plenty of natural light often feels much nicer than its opposite and lures tenants and purchasers like moths to a flame.

We all need air to live. The better the property's **ventilation**, the nicer your experience in the property. Poorly ventilated properties often carry a smell and don't feel nice to live in. A property with cross-flow ventilation stays cooler in the warmer months and can feel larger than it is.

Even small properties can be designed to feel more open. An open kitchen, living and outdoor entertaining area makes a place feel larger, welcoming and communal. People highly value **open space**, and properties that feel tight or poky are normally severely penalised in growth over the long term.

Privacy and security are two fundamental needs of almost all people. These attributes are achieved through a variety of means, such as secure entrances, sturdy building materials, property location and orientation, man-made or natural screening, and technology: intercoms, lock-up garages, cameras and security systems are all valuable characteristics. The sense of security is a strong emotional trigger that makes all the difference for some tenants and purchasers.

Views – whether they are of water, trees, mountains, a cityscape or parklands – are always valuable. Such views can provide a sense of peace or entertainment and deliver higher value than a view of a wall or fence. Your tastes and lifestyle will determine how much of a premium you are willing to pay but, as an investment, you can be certain that there will always be a market for this attribute. A view is only accessible from certain locations, and this scarcity makes it unique and valuable. Whether you are buying a home or an investment, it is often a good idea to seek out this attribute if you can afford it.

What the **building** is made of, its age, the fixtures, the fittings and the aesthetic all impact the value of the property as an investment in the years to come. These features also determine how comfortable you or your tenants will be, the longevity of the property and the maintenance required for the property to function well. Though a depreciating asset, the value of the building cannot be understated. The replacement cost of some structures can be tremendous, and there may be a lot of opportunities for the aspiring property developer to make structural or cosmetic upgrades that add value to the property and make for a great investment.

Location is one of the most important attributes of a property, if not the most important. Where is the property is located relative to other properties, amenities and infrastructure impacts your standard of living and the value of your investment in a huge way. It is often better to have the worst property in the best street than the best property in a bad street. You can always improve the property, but you can't improve the location. There is a lot of value in your property being close to more valuable homes because these homes lift the value of the area as a whole.

Size matters. All things being equal, when it comes to real estate, bigger is generally better. There are diminishing returns at a point, but having more land or more internal square metres gives you options. If you own more land, there may be an opportunity to cut it up into smaller parcels. A bigger apartment may allow you to add another bedroom or do some significant renovations. Aside from these improvements, people will always favour a little extra space. However, the key thing to remember here is that you want usable space. For example, you may be comparing two apartments side by side and notice that one has more internal floor area than the other, but the bigger apartment may have a long hallway that doesn't really add any value, and after you remove that from the calculations the other apartment may actually be the better option.

Paper attributes

Paper attributes are those characteristics of the property that help you to assess its value and performance as an investment. Even if you are buying a property as your home, it is important to note how it might perform as an investment and familiarise yourself with some of the following attributes.

Yield is the amount of rent received divided by the amount you paid for the investment. For example, if a property cost you $500,000 and you receive $25,000 in rent per annum, your gross yield would be 5 per cent (because 25,000 divided by 500,000 equals 0.05). A higher yield means better cash flow from the property. Cash flow investors who want their expenses paid by the investment chase strong yields. However, this can come at the cost of growth from the property or a bunch of headaches. This is typically because good properties have lower yields; higher yields come from properties that are riskier.

Properties in rural areas provide an example of this. Rural areas might have properties for sale for as low as $350,000 because fewer people are willing to buy this type of property – that rent for $400 per week, which means the rent is strong relative to the price (almost 6 per cent in this case). However, because the area is very affordable, it will attract people from lower socio-economic situations, which means a greater chance of problematic tenants. While these properties have strong yields, this can come at the cost of chasing tenants for rent and constantly needing to fix things. On the other hand, a nice property that costs $6 million might rent for $2500 per week, which is less than 2.2 per cent rental yield. This may be a highly desirable property to own but there are not as many people who can afford to rent it; and, since it has a low yield, it will cost you a lot of money annually to hold it and hope for growth.

The **vacancy rate** is the percentage of properties in the area you are looking to buy in that are likely to be vacant or empty. It is the average rate for all the real estate in the area; so, when using it, make sure you note whether your property is below or above average quality for the area. If your property is much better than the others in the market and you are looking for fair market rent, then your property is likely to be vacant for less than the average amount of time. Note that an area's vacancy rate assumes market rent; so, if you are nervous about your property being empty, you can always discount the rent and make your property more likely to be rented quickly.

How a property is zoned determines what you can do with it. Each state and suburb has different **zoning** laws and regulations that need to be thoroughly reviewed before you make any decisions about buying a property for the purposes of development, subdivision or major renovations. The zoning of land can affect the price of a property tremendously, since it impacts what can be done on that block of land. This is relevant for houses, townhouses and apartments because a shift from lower to higher density allows developers to step in and profit from these changes. Homebuyers who find a great home with zoning that allows for development need to be prepared to pay a premium.

The **height limit** of the land that you are looking to buy determines how many levels or metres your property can be built to. This is a handy piece of information if you are looking to do renovations or develop a block of land or house. If the block has a three-storey height limit and the existing house is only one storey, you have the capacity to add a couple of floors and, depending on the location, take advantage of views or an outlook. This type of renovation can add a huge amount of value to your home or investment.

The **minimum lot size** is most relevant to property buyers with intentions of doing a development or subdividing a block of land. Parcels of land generally have rules around the minimum size that a block can be. When buying a bigger block, part of the attraction for investors is the ability to cut this larger block into smaller pieces to make a profit.

Covenants and easements are effectively restrictions and obligations over a property. A covenant is a legally binding agreement placed on a private property to protect, preserve and sometimes enhance specific features. There are several different types of covenants that relate to the environment, water, animals and landscape. An easement is a right attached to land that gives a party (such as the government or a neighbour) the right to use the land for a specific purpose even though the property belongs to you. Common examples of this include drainage, sewerage and access easements, but there are others that may be more prohibitive. It is important to understand what covenants and easements exist on a property before buying because they may have a very big impact on what you can do from a building point of view.

How to not f*ck it up

There are a few key ways to not f*ck up the selection of your property:

- *Be clear on what you want:* Reference the previous two chapters in this book. Being clear on what you want and setting out your criteria will give you laser-like focus when hunting for your property. Prioritising these characteristics will ensure that they align with your goal and will make sure you don't get confused and buy something you regret.

- *Do your checks:* The next chapter covers how to secure your property. However, I noted previously that there are certain paper attributes you should be clear on before purchasing. Doing these checks with your solicitor will ensure you don't make a severe mistake by buying something with the wrong zoning or with detrimental covenants and easements.

- *Look for something unique:* A property that has unique, valuable characteristics will increase in value in the years to come at a greater rate than other properties. You want to compare the property that you intend on buying against the rest of the market and see if there are features that make it stand out from the rest.

Chapter 10

Secure Your Investment

You have done the research and found the area you like and the property that you want to buy. Now it is time to secure your property and do all the last-minute checks to make sure it is everything that you want it to be.

Securing your property is the process of ordering the contract, checking the obvious details (such as your name and property address), and then signing and dating it and paying your deposit. It may sound silly but, when ordering your contract, make sure the sales advice (the document ordering your contract) has the correct spelling and full names of all the people or entities that will be entering into the contract. This will save you a lot of time and potential heartache later, especially when you are getting your finance organised. I have worked with people of many different nationalities and know that some cultures have lots of names and different naming conventions, so make sure all names are on there.

The next simple thing for you to do is to check that the property details listed on the contract match the property that you are buying. Yes, it sounds silly, but silly mistakes do happen; just because a property is marketed a certain way does not mean that it has been marketed correctly. This was almost the first mistake I made when buying my first property: the agent had marketed the property as having 89 square metres of internal space, and it wasn't until I did my contract review that I noticed the apartment had 89 square metres of total space and only 70 square metres internally. You can find this sort of information on the provided title or strata plans.

Another detail you may miss is all of the checkboxes on the front page of your contract, or an attached schedule of inclusions. Your contract will detail what is and is not included in the sale of the property. Make sure everything that was promised to you by the agent and seller is noted in the contract. It is not uncommon for people to say you will get certain inclusions with the property – or even certain exclusions – that are not noted in the contract. If you are one of those bargain-hunter property buyers, some properties may come with a whole bunch of rubbish you would like removed before you take ownership of your investment.

At this stage, it is vitally important to have a great solicitor or conveyancer who understands all the legal terms and conditions that make up the property contract. The legal representative is there to translate the contract into simple, easy-to-understand English, negotiate favourable terms for you and reduce any potential risks. You want the solicitor to point out or remove anything onerous in the contract, taking every possible step to ensure your security!

How to not f*ck it up

The most important way to not f*ck up your contract is to simply get legal representation, and do not get the cheapest solution that you can find! I have seen firsthand what happens when clients go for the cheaper option here: it can cost you heartache, time and tens of thousands of dollars. You are making one of the most expensive purchases of your life; invest the time and money into good legal representation and advice.

Now that we have established the first cardinal rule, we can jump into some other important pieces of information. I won't bore you with all the potential legal terms and conditions in a contract to be aware of; instead, following are a couple of questions to ask to help you pick the right legal representative.

First, however, let's clarify the difference between a solicitor and a conveyancer. The main difference is that a conveyancer is a specialist in the transfer of ownership of property between parties, whereas a lawyer can do much more than this. For the purposes of a contract review, either will suffice, but some people prefer to use solicitors because they have a wider base of knowledge.

So, here are two important questions for you to ask your legal representative.

How long have you been doing this for?

You want someone with years of experience on your side who has seen a broad variety of real estate deals. Having a junior with limited experience can be problematic when your property is not vanilla and has terms and conditions, covenants and easements that they are not familiar with. An inexperienced solicitor or conveyancer may give you the wrong advice and talk you out of a deal that could be very lucrative simply because they don't feel comfortable with the contract, or they may push too hard on terms that may not be very important and ruin the deal. The reverse can also happen, and they may miss or not fully understand the risks in the contract and advise that it is safe for you to continue with your purchase when it is not.

What type of properties do you normally work on?

People often assume that all real estate contracts are the same. They are not. Properties on the open market have different contracts to properties that are bought off the plan or are being constructed as part of a house-and-land package. It is important to know that your legal representative has experience with the type of property you are buying. If they don't, this can become problematic because they may give you the wrong impression of the contract and its contents. Off-the-plan properties have very different contracts to properties bought on the market; they are generally bigger and make allowances for a number of other parties, such as the developer's bank, and have conditions that will not be present in other contracts. A solicitor or conveyancer who is not familiar with all of this may advise against buying this type of property without knowing your reasons for wanting to proceed, causing you unnecessary fear.

PART III

The Philosophy

In this third and final section of the book, I unpack some of the philosophy around investing in real estate, as well as some strategies and ways of thinking about real estate that have served me well along the way. It is my hope that you might pick up one or two new ideas to make buying property less stressful and more profitable for you.

There are different schools of thought about how to buy and make money in property. If you have not already read other investment books, after this one you will likely venture into the world of real estate investment advice and come across other authors and thought leaders with different ideas. You will also encounter many friends, family and strangers with strong property investment philosophies who insist that their way is the best. What you may have noticed in this book is that I have mentioned a range of different ways to invest and make money in property.

The truth is that all these different schools of investing work. It just comes down to the execution, and what most people avoid saying is that it also helps to have a little luck. This comes back to the first chapter and my boss's old saying: 'Investing in property is easy, you just need to not f*ck it up'. The not-so-secret secret is that you just need to hold the property for long enough and you will eventually get lucky.

Let's talk about property philosophy.

Chapter 11

Strategies

I have touched on many different ways to invest in real estate throughout this book. In this chapter I list some of the main ways to profit off this investment class and highlight some of the risks.

Before we dive into the details, let's cover one of the most important principles that will help you decide which strategy suits you, your goals, your lifestyle and your risk appetite the most: I call it the profit–pain principle.

The profit–pain principle

As the name suggests, the more profit you want to make, the more pain you are likely to experience. This is not to say that all painful deals are profitable, or that all profitable deals have to be painful. It is a simple principle to help you think about your investment style and rationalise the type of investment you would like to make. I reference this principle throughout this chapter as we explore the different strategies you can use when investing in real estate.

Figure 3, over the page, illustrates the principle simply.

Figure 3: The profit–pain principle

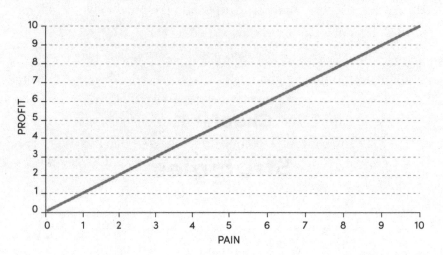

Profit is the money that you can make out of the deal. Pain is whatever you need to do or experience to complete the deal and get your profit. Pain can include money paid out, time you have to use up and effort that you have to invest in the property, as well as the stress you feel while doing the deal. If you are putting in little money, time or effort, you are not likely to get much of a return on your investment.

Home or investment?

The first big question almost all property buyers ask themselves is this: *Should I buy my own home or an investment?* Both make for good options but for different reasons. The biggest problems occur when people do as they have been told without really thinking about what suits them best.

For some people this question is actually really tough because there is so much emotion built into it. Unless you work in the real estate or investment industry, it's likely that all you have learnt about property so far has come from your parents, other family members and, to a lesser extent, your friends. The problem with this is that these trusted people are not experts and are only going to tell you what they have learnt from their experience. Some of this is valuable information but much is not, because their experiences and situation in life are not yours.

People who bought property before 1992 were very fortunate on the property front. The Australian property market grew by about 381.2 per cent between December 1991 and December 2021. This means that the median dwelling value across the country rose from $114,034 to $709,803 over that period. That median dwelling value in December 1991 would have gotten you a decent house in a location not far from a major metro hub and, since debt was so expensive, your best bet was to pay it down as fast as you could.

We now live in a different time. It costs you more to buy less, and your income proportional to property prices and debt is also significantly smaller than it was back then. Many people who bought their houses 30 years ago (at the time of writing) are still living in them. The generation buying properties now are much more mobile and transitory, interest rates are much lower, the world works differently and information is readily available for those willing to look. The great thing about the first property you buy is that it does not need to be your last but rather can be a means to buy your second, or potentially your shortcut to buying the home you really want.

Buying your own home or an investment comes with pros and cons, and each comes with different strategies. Let's take a look.

Buying your own home

Australians culturally want to buy their own home. They want their own place, where they can put nails in the walls to hang photos up, where they can nest and feel secure. For many people this desire to buy their own home has been inherited rather than carefully thought out to see if it actually serves their interests and lifestyle. Buying your own home can be great, but it can also be a massive burden that brings more pain than gain. I think buying your own home is a great goal and can be extremely beneficial at certain times in your life, but it is not the answer for all people all the time.

Let's look at the pros of buying your own home.

The first pro is **emotion**. It feels good to own your own home and be paying down something that is yours. Walking around the property and enjoying your bit of grass or your view feels really good, and it is nice to know that it cannot be taken away from you. The goal to pay off your mortgage and own your home outright is easy to understand and a good way to ensure a stable future. At the right time in your life, buying your home will also give you a sense of relief at having achieved the goal you have set for yourself.

There is an added sense of **stability** that comes from owning a home. For people with kids, stability is important. Families want a reliable routine and the security of knowing that their children are committed to a school, they can make friends locally and there is no fear of being forced to move. Owning your home brings simplicity. There is little to manage and the goal is clear: keep the family happy and pay down the debt. For some people this sense of stability is priceless.

Owning your home also comes with the benefit of **customisation**. It is your home, so you can do what you want (provided it complies with council regulations) – unlike a rental property, where you take the property as it is. You can customise your own home as much as you like and tailor it to your wants and needs.

After living in your home for a while (check with your accountant to see how long 'a while' is), you can sell your home and pay no **capital gains tax** (CGT). This can save you hundreds of thousands of dollars and change your life in a meaningful way.

Buying your own home also gives you access to **the house-flipping strategy**. The tax benefits of flipping your own home are huge (in terms of the CGT just mentioned), but this investment strategy is not without a lot of risk and comes with a lot of pain. Flipping homes successfully requires a good eye for property. You also need to have a strong understanding of building, design and the property market. It requires a lot of cash to do the building and good cash flow to keep you afloat while your home is under construction. Doing construction on the home you are living in can be a very painful and expensive experience, and you will learn a lot of hard lessons the first few times you do it. Depending on how often you plan on flipping homes, it can also be very disruptive to your family. I would give this strategy a profit–pain score of 9 out of 10: you can make a lot of money, but it will come at the cost of a lot of pain.

How to not f*ck it up

If you feel that the house-flipping strategy strategy might be for you, here are a few ways to not f*ck it up:

- *Start small:* Work on a project that requires minimal structural work and mostly cosmetic work, such as painting walls, putting in new floors or updating kitchen cupboards, hardware and some landscaping. You will learn a lot from doing small projects, and they are a good way to get some cash flow going.
- *Research:* Read books in this space, watch YouTube videos, join forums and learn from people who have done it, including the professionals. There are a lot of good resources on how to flip homes well that will save you a lot of time and money.
- *Get help:* Recruit all the help that you can get. You will likely have friends, family and other people in your extended network

who are tradespeople or who work in the space. It is good to have people around you who you trust and can rely upon for good advice.

- *Do not rush:* Haste makes waste. Plan your project thoroughly and avoid having to rush to get work done. If you slow down and plan what you need to do prior to starting your project, you will often save time and money down the road. When you rush, you make poor decisions, and you will often make mistakes and spend more money than necessary.

Following are some of the cons of buying your own home.

It is likely that the home you are going to buy is not really what you want, and you will have to **compromise** on price, location, size, quality, lifestyle or many other factors. This is especially true for your first property. Many people compromise on price by stretching too far and putting undue pressure on themselves and their family, or they compromise on lifestyle and buy within their means, which is great, but in a less-than-ideal situation simply so they can say they are living in their property. Buying your own home can come with extreme sacrifices that you simply do not need to make.

Buying your own home typically means that you will receive **no income** from the property, unless you are renting out some of the space in your house, such as a room or granny flat. Having no income from the property makes it harder to hold the asset over a long period of time, and renting out some space means you are compromising your privacy and peace of mind.

Lack of income is one of the biggest ways people get into trouble with owning their own home. It means you are dependent on the household income, which can change due to sickness, pregnancy or economic conditions. When you cannot meet your repayments, banks can step in and force you to sell the asset, and you have little to no control over what price you get for it.

Another downside has to do with **tax**. Unlike with investment properties, none of the interest and expenses on your own home are tax deductible. This means that all the costs come out of your pocket, and there are no end-of-financial-year tax refunds to put more money into your account.

Buying your own home means you are committed. It can be difficult, slow and expensive to sell a property; so, once you have made the **commitment** to buy a home and live in it, that's the strategy for a while, unless you are willing to take on the pain and sacrifice of changing course midway through your strategy. Yes, you can later rent the property out as an investment, but it may not be a very good investment, or the rental return may be terrible relative to other investments you could have bought.

Buying an investment property

Residential real estate accounts for about 57 per cent of Australians' household wealth and, at an approximate total value of $9.7 trillion, is worth more than all Australian listed stocks, superannuation and commercial real estate combined. Buying real estate as an investment can be daunting at first but it can be extremely fulfilling once it is done. When it is done right – that is, when the property meets your budget and strategy – it can be a seamless process with lots of rewards and only the occasional headache. Investing in property can take many forms and, depending on your strategy, could take little to no effort or monumental effort, but the rewards will match this effort more often than not. Once you start investing, it will become addictive and life-changing.

When it is done right, investing in real estate is very **rewarding**. There is a learning curve and a significant monetary hurdle to start but, once you get going, it gets easier and there are almost unlimited opportunities for you to change your life. Depending on your pain threshold, there are several ways to invest, each of which will attract a different return. Most people will buy one property plus their own home and, after a couple of decades, pay them down and live off the passive income. This is a simple and effective way to become financially free. Other people start off with one property and keep on investing to build huge fortunes.

Property is the biggest asset class in the world – everyone needs a roof over their head, so you will always have a captive market. For the few investors who commit to learning about investing in real estate, it can supercharge their wealth creation, give them a career in managing and building their portfolio and liberate them from the previous version of their life.

Real estate gives you an **income**. Depending on how much debt you have and your property expenses, some properties will passively pay you an income every single month without you having to put in much or any effort. I have never been a very good saver, so seeing my bank accounts grow from my properties was life-changing for me. I started as a bit of a lazy investor who did not want too much pain, so it was extremely satisfying to have a portfolio that worked while I didn't and filled my bank accounts every single month.

This income gave me the confidence to make decisions that I may not have without that extra support. An example of this is that I left my old job to start a business. My passive income and growing portfolio felt like my parachute after taking this leap of faith. If I'd owned my own home that required me to make repayments on my loan, that may have been too much stress for me to start the business. I would have gone from having a healthy salary to earning nothing. Having a passive income is life-changing and a worthy pursuit if your goal is to be free of financial commitments.

The Australian government incentivises its citizens to own investment properties through **tax deductions**. All the expenses – including but not limited to agent fees, strata, rates, repairs, depreciation and interest on your loan – are tax deductible. To put it simply, you can claim all these expenses to reduce the income you earn through the year.

This is going to be a simplistic explanation – there are other books that you can read on this, or you can visit my Wealthi Academy – but let's say you are earning $100,000 and your rental income is $25,000. Your total income for the year would be $125,000. Now let's assume that all the expenses I just listed amounted to $45,000 for the year; this would mean that your taxable income is now $125,000 minus $45,000, which is $80,000. The tax you pay on $80,000 is less than on your original $100,000, which means that, after your accountant has lodged your tax return, you should be getting a refund. Some properties, such as new investments, are better for tax purposes than others, but this does not necessarily mean they make for better investments. You never want to invest purely to save on tax, but it certainly should factor into your decision-making, since it is a big incentive and can make a huge difference to the cost of running your property.

You also get access to **the rentvesting strategy**. Living where you want and investing where you can afford is a great strategy to live life on your terms and use the Australian tax system to your advantage. A lot of people who want to buy their own home will say, 'I hate paying rent, it is dead money'. To them I say it is OK to pay rent if you are also collecting it. The additional benefit here is that nicer properties typically have lower yields (the amount of rent you receive proportional to the price of the property), and investment properties have tax benefits that make them cheaper to own than your own home. This is a very common strategy among property investors because it gives them the freedom to move around easily, upgrade their home on demand and build a property portfolio to suit their strategy. I used this strategy for more than a decade before choosing to buy my own home. Yes, just because you use this strategy for a while does not mean you need to do it forever. In fact, many people would say it is the easiest, cheapest and fastest way to buy the home you actually want. The rentvesting strategy gives you flexibility over your income and lifestyle while making you money and creating equity in your portfolio.

I would give rentvesting a profit–pain score of 7 out of 10. Renting and investing can be extremely profitable, especially if you count all the tax deductions and are strategic about your lifestyle choices and investment loan structures. However, it comes with the pain of being a little uncertain about where you are going to live in the long term. If you are not used to having a lease and this brings you stress, this may be more painful to you than others. On the other hand, if you are accustomed to having a lease and are happy to move around, this strategy may not be very painful for you at all.

The main downside of buying an investment property is **stress**. Investing is inherently stressful. You are moving your life's savings from your bank – where there is little to no risk (except for inflation) – and buying a property, acquiring debt, collecting rent, paying costs and managing an asset. Depending on your strategy and the property you buy, this can mean a little stress or lots. Investing requires you to spend time and effort learning about something new and there are a number of moving parts that you add to your life. Depending on the level of complexity, this can become very stressful, and many people would much rather have a simpler, less stressful experience. The leads some to buy easy-to-manage, simple investments or their own home.

The key thing to remember here is that stress is not necessarily a bad thing. It usually means you are outside of your comfort zone and growing. The more time you spend here, the less stressful things become, since you learn to manage more complex scenarios over time. When it comes to investing, this typically means you can make more money.

New property

New property comes in many shapes and sizes. You can buy something off the plan or that has been newly completed, or you can construct a property yourself. As covered in previous chapters, you can choose the new property strategy to build wealth, and it is one of the simplest and least painful ways to invest in real estate.

New property is great for amateur property investors. It requires little to no maintenance and repairs, attracts a better selection of tenants, allows for staggered or delayed payment of deposits and allows tax deductions from depreciation to reduce your tax liability. However, it is also more expensive than existing property and relies upon the market to do a lot of the equity creation for you.

I would give new property a profit–pain score of 7 out of 10. It can be very profitable but comes with the pain of uncertainty. Since many new properties are bought off the plan, you do not get the luxury of seeing what you are getting, and you normally have to wait a while before taking ownership of the property. The reason the score is not higher is because much of the risk is being taken on by the people developing the property for you. New property is also relatively easy to manage after you take ownership because property managers take over and you should not hear from them about issues with the property.

Existing property

Existing property – buying a property in the open market with warts and all – is one of the most common ways to invest in real estate.

Every property is unique and comes in a different state of repair. Generally, the older the property and the more work you need to do to it, the cheaper it will be and the more value you will be able to create for yourself. This is an attractive way to invest that gives you more control over the pain and profitability of your property.

Existing property is good for more experienced investors. It allows you to plan for most of your problems (because what you see is what you get), makes it possible to find bargains and gives you some control over the profits you can make to accelerate your growth. You can do a deal here and now to get immediate benefit. However, it requires a significant commitment of time, effort and cash or equity.

I would give existing property a profit–pain score of 8.5 out of 10. Buying property on the open market comes with some risks, but these risks also represent opportunities. For example, after you have bought a property, it may require some work before you can rent it back out again. The work can be as simple as repainting and replacing the carpet, which is fast, cheap and easy to do. This work may add a little value to the property and get you some more rent. A more complex job such as rebuilding kitchens and bathrooms is expensive and takes lots of time and experience to do well, but the benefits can be tremendous – you can add tens of thousands of dollars of value to your property and attract a lot of extra rent. With more control comes greater complexity and potential profit.

Property development

Property development is an industry, a profession and a way to invest. This is by far the most painful and profitable way to invest in real estate. There are many books, lectures, podcasts and videos that you can learn from and still not know enough to fully understand it without getting in and learning from experience. It is generally very expensive to get started unless you are willing to commit a lot of time and work to learning about deal making, commercial transactions, investors and contracts. This is a very attractive way to accelerate your wealth creation, but it carries with it a lot of risk. It is suited to experienced property investors.

I would give property development a profit–pain score of 10 out of 10. For those willing to work hard, property development can be very rewarding, but it comes with a lot of risk. The benefit of dealing with property is that, the more you work on it, the more experience you collect, and over time you mature into an experienced investor. The first few investments may be simple and profitable, which allows you to dive into further complexity as you go along. After making some money, you might choose to develop your own property after 5, 10, 15 or 20 years. There are safe ways to do this, but it just takes time, money and experience.

For those looking to get started, Ron Forlee wrote a great book called *Australian Residential Property Development for Investors*.

Regional property

Regional property is a hotly contested topic among many real estate investors. Investing in regional cities and towns has always been alluring due to their affordability, size and rental returns. You simply get more bang for your buck, and since the huge returns that followed COVID-19 it has gotten even more popular.

Historically, properties across Australia's capital cities combined increased 414.9 per cent in value over the 30 years prior to 2022, compared to 278 per cent in the combined regions. The 30-year annualised growth was 5.6 per cent across the combined capitals and 4.5 per cent across the combined regional market. This is not to say that regional cities do not make for good growth investments, but you need to be more strategic with what you invest in, since the chances are that you'd be better off buying in capital cities if your goal is to create equity.

I have invested in both capital cities and regional markets. Both have performed very well but, in every instance, I was strategic about what I was buying. As noted in previous chapters, my rule of thumb when investing in regional cities is that they need to have a thriving economic centre with good infrastructure, a big population that is growing and a wide variety of employment opportunities. The bigger the population, the more stable and liquid the property market will be; I normally look for cities with more than 50,000 people. This is not to say that I would not look at cities with fewer people, but the deal would need to be much more attractive.

With regional property, it is cheaper to enter the market, you can buy bigger properties for less money and you can achieve more attractive yields and, therefore, cash flow. However, they are historically riskier than the capital cities and can be more volatile and harder to exit.

I would give regional property a profit–pain score of 6 out of 10. Because it is much cheaper to buy in regional markets and the cash flow is generally better than in the cities, I consider buying regionally to be a simple strategy. Some markets are very risky and have big returns, but the fact you can make much smaller investments makes it easy to get started. Generally, the returns – and, hence, the profitability – have been lower.

COVID-19 has changed some things about buying regional markets, the big thing being the increase in people working from home. In the last census it came to light that 21 per cent of all employed people in Australia worked at home on Census Day 2021, almost five times the number in 2016. It looks like this is a big systemic change that is not likely to go away. Just because the regional market has performed one way for the past 30 years, this is not to say it will continue this way; it may perform better going into the future.

Commercial property

The risk in commercial property relative to residential comes from the fact that not everyone needs to run a business but everyone needs a roof over their heads to live. Commercial property is more complex than residential property, but it can be simple to manage once you know the ropes. It is suited to more sophisticated investors. It is generally a great way to create a passive income – it provides strong cash flow and the security of long-term leases. However, it also requires bigger deposits, lower loan-to-value ratios and a more in-depth understanding of finance, leases and contracts because there are more variables to negotiate than with residential real estate. Growth in value is typically linked to the rental returns and the tenant – the higher the yield, the riskier the property, tenant and terms.

I would give commercial property a profit–pain score of 9 out of 10. It is a very lucrative market that many sophisticated investors tend to gravitate towards because the rental returns are normally much stronger than with residential property and the tenancy agreements are longer. However, there is a great deal of risk that comes from the finance structure, tenancy terms and tenant profile. It is very common for commercial properties to have times when they are difficult to rent out and are vacant for long periods, especially relative to residential properties. It is a great asset class for investors who are looking to create a strong passive income, but it is best suited to people who have some experience in property and plenty of cash or equity in the bank. (A strong position would be about 30 per cent of the property's value.)

How to not f*ck it up

The best way to avoid making a poor decision about the type of property you buy is to be clear on how much pain you are willing to undertake to make a profit – not the other way around. People who become captivated by chasing profits often fall into traps of their own creation, since they are blinded to the burdens that this path brings. The problem is that, once you have committed to a course of action, it is very difficult to stop halfway without taking a loss. Buying a property is a big decision with a lot of moving parts and things that can go wrong. Typically, the more complicated the deal, the more profitable it is, but also the riskier it is.

Know your limits and work just outside of your comfort zone. As your experience grows, so too will your comfort zone, and you can then push a little more. The patient game wins when making money in real estate.

Chapter 12

Final Considerations

Buying property is always a big deal, whether it is your first, fifth or tenth investment. With each subsequent purchase, it gets easier in some ways and harder in others. In addition to the topics covered throughout the rest of this book, here are a few more points for consideration when buying your next property.

Cash flow versus growth

The idea that you have to choose between strong cash flow and strong growth is a very big generalisation. Some properties achieve both from the beginning and, if given enough time, most properties will eventually provide you with strong cash flow as well as growth. After ten years, if you have not 'f*cked it up', your property of choice should have a huge amount of equity and, if it is an investment, your rent should have grown by at least the value of inflation and maybe more. Over this period of time most people would have paid off some of their debt, and for others the rent might simply have grown fast enough to cover all their expenses and pay some extra income each month.

This generalisation exists because many of the best-performing growth markets have lower yields than more affordable and riskier locations. In the short to medium term, it is important to have a very clear understanding of your budget to know how much you can afford to pay towards your property each month, since this will provide you with clarity about the property you want to buy.

As a rule of thumb, properties with positive cash flow are great because you can leave them to grow indefinitely, but they may not grow very much in value. For example, you may have bought a $500,000 property that makes you $100 per week but that only grows by 20 per cent ($100,000) over ten years. In that time, you've made $5200 per year, which is $52,000 over ten years. Add the $100,000 in growth and that's $252,000 in total. Another $500,000 property might *cost* you $5200 per year but grow by 80 per cent ($400,000) over the ten years; subtract the $52,000 cost to hold over ten years from the $400,000 growth and you're left with $348,000 total profit.

Comparing these two examples, it makes more sense to buy the property that costs you money every year because the total return is better. The risk, though, is that some properties may cost you money every year and still not grow much in value. Some people might still prefer the first property even though the total return is worse because they cannot afford – or do not want to pay – annual out-of-pocket expenses. This is why it is so important to know how much risk you are willing to take and how much you can afford to pay for a property up-front and ongoing, as well as to have a good understanding of what the 10-, 20- and 30-year exit strategy looks like for you.

It is never going to be perfect

Your first property will not tick all the boxes; in fact, your second, third and fourth may not either. It is important to recognise that these properties you buy are never going to be perfect, but you will find something in them that will get the job done. As noted in previous chapters, you want to choose a property that ticks your must-have boxes, and it is a bonus if it meets some of your want-to-have criteria. Treat each property as an investment and business decision even if it is going to be your home. List what you want to achieve, rank your needs and pick the property that hits most of your key criteria, and then move on.

If you hold out for something that is perfect, you'll end up sitting on the sidelines doing nothing, or you'll go the other way and overanalyse everything. This is a huge problem because it can cause decision fatigue, make you confused and result in you just choosing something for the sake of being done. Agents know this; it is one of the reasons why they ask how long you have been looking for your property.

When to use your head or your heart

Buying a property is always going to stir up an emotional response. It is hard to not have an emotional response to spending $200 on shoes, let alone $500,000 on a life-changing investment. The trick here is to know when to use your emotions and when to ignore them.

Use your emotions to stir you into action, save up your money, engage some professionals to help and persevere when times get tough. Use your emotions when seeing and thinking about property. It is good when a property stirs positive emotional responses in you because of the view, the location or the amenities, since your tenant and future buyers will likely have a similar experience. People pay more for things that stir positive emotional responses and, if their emotions get carried away, you are more likely to get a higher price when you sell or rent out the property.

Do not use your emotions when thinking strategically, doing the maths on your property or making logical decisions. You do not need to love all your investments; you are not likely to ever live in them. They are for someone else to live in and to make you money.

Be very careful if you have fallen in love with a property and find yourself painting grand visions for the future for you and your family. The more emotion you put into this property, the higher the price you are likely to pay, and this can cost you greatly in the future. Those rose-coloured glasses will often cause you to miss detrimental details that you simply did not consider because you wanted to make the property work. Remember to always come back to your key criteria and your budget.

There is a fine balance to strike between your head and your heart when buying real estate, so it is always helpful to get advice from people who are not emotionally connected to your decision-making process.

Buying with friends and family

It can be very tempting to buy property with your closest friends and family. It can be very beneficial to all parties, since it allows you to get into the property market faster or buy something bigger than you could afford alone. There are many ways to buy property with people and they all have their pros and cons. Let's look at a few of them very briefly, along with some ideas to consider before you make this big decision. One thing to note is that you should seek professional advice from an accountant and a solicitor before committing to any of these structures so that you deeply understand the implications.

- *Joint tenants:* This is where each person owns an equal share of the asset. Most couples buy property like this since the property can be passed to the other person in matters of the estate if someone passes. However, it can be complicated if you want to sell your 'share'.

- *Tenants in common:* This is a type of ownership that allows people to buy and own unequal shares of an asset. If one of the owners dies, their share gets administered by their will and estate. This type of ownership allows for tax planning and different ownership structures. For instance, you can own a property with a 99 per cent to 1 per cent split, or 70 per cent to 30 per cent. This flexibility makes this structure a common choice for friends, couples in new relationships and people enacting clever tax accounting schemes.

- *Trusts:* This is where things get much more complicated from an ownership and finance perspective. You will need professional advice when setting up these structures since there are a wide variety of ways to do this. Put simply, you are setting up an entity that you and your friends or family buy a share in. This entity goes out to get the finance and buy the property. People like this structure because it is easier to sell your share in the entity and manage the investment.

Here are a few things to consider before you buy a property with other people:

- *Management:* There is some work that goes into buying and managing a property, so you need to be clear on who is doing this and whether they will be paid for it.

- *Goals:* What are you trying to achieve when buying this property, and at what point are you happy to sell it or refinance it to get more debt?

- *Exit:* As life goes on, things change – people have babies, travel and want different things. What happens if someone wants to get out of the property?

The bottom line is that buying property is a big and expensive decision that comes with lots of moving parts and emotions. Everyone is different and, when you start to involve money in family and friendships, things change. I have always told my clients that, if you can afford to buy a property buy yourself, do it that way. It is better to have 100 per cent control over your assets than to have a share. Things get much more complicated when you involve other people.

Think big, start small and grow consistently

'Think big, start small and grow consistently' is a little mantra that we often say at Wealthi. It is a reminder to all of us to have big aspirations but not get too daunted by how we'll achieve them, since it all starts with a small first step. The little step forward is easy to take and, if small steps are taken consistently, they will eventually lead you to achieve your big visions for the future.

One thing that has always surprised me about people is our ability to just get things done. After you have put pen to paper and set a goal, your mind conspires to get it done both consciously and subconsciously. Now that I recognise this, I have learnt not to sell myself short – to aim for bigger goals and not get too caught up in how I will get it all done. For me it is more important to start moving in the right direction and fall in love with the process of moving in that direction every day.

How to not f*ck it up

Be open to new ideas, ways of thinking and investing. There is no best way to do things. In truth, all the strategies and philosophes covered in this book work – it just comes down to what you want to achieve. The one truth that I have learnt above all else is not to rush into anything you do not understand, but also to not wait to know it all before you take that leap of faith. You will never know it all and this can drive you crazy, but you can know enough to make an educated decision. Property is a game of patience and rewards people who get in early, consistently learn and add to their portfolio over time.

I hope reading this book is your small action that leads to your much bigger visions for the future.

Good luck and happy investing.

Glossary

APRA. Australian Prudential Regulation Authority, the regulator of the Australian financial services sector.

Body corporate. The governing body of a block of apartments or townhouses. They manage the common areas.

Cash flow. The difference between an investment property's rental income and expenses. A property with positive cash flow earns more in rental income than it costs to hold (in terms of mortgage repayments, maintenance and so on).

CGT. Capital gains tax, the tax you pay on the profit when you sell an investment property.

Conveyancer. A specialist in the transfer of property ownership between parties.

Covenant. A legally binding restriction placed on a property that determines how it can be used or developed.

DTI. Debt-to-income ratio, a measure of how much debt you can service on your income. For example, a DTI of 1:6 on an income of $100,000 per year means you can get a loan of $600,000.

Easement. A legal right to use someone else's land for a specific, limited purpose: for example: drainage, sewerage or access.

Equity. The value of your ownership of a property. For example, if you have a property valued at $600,000 and a mortgage of $400,000, then you have $200,000 or 40 per cent equity in that property.

Flipping. An investing strategy whereby you renovate a property and then sell it for more than the cost of the renovations.

Full doc. Full documentation, a type of loan that requires you to provide comprehensive documentation to the lender in order to secure the loan. This is generally rewarded with a lower rate of interest than for a 'low doc' loan.

Gentrification. The process of wealthier people moving into an area and raising the socioeconomic status of the area.

IO. Interest only, a type of loan whereby your repayments cover only the interest on the loan and you do not pay down any of the principal.

Joint tenants. A form of ownership in which multiple people own an equal share of a property.

LMI. Lenders mortgage insurance, which protects the insurer from financial loss if you are unable to meet your home loan repayments. Commonly, you are required to pay LMI if your LVR is lower than 80 per cent.

Low doc. Low documentation, a type of loan that requires you to provide relatively little documentation to the lender in order to secure the loan. This is generally compensated for by a higher rate of interest.

LVR. Loan-to-value ratio, the ratio of the size of your loan versus the value of the property. For example, if you have an LVR of 80 per cent, the size of your loan is 80 per cent of the value of the property.

Overcapitalisation. When you spend more money upgrading a property than you gain in value from the upgrade.

Owners' corporation. *See body corporate.*

P&I. Principal and interest, a type of loan whereby your repayments cover both the interest (the fee you pay to the bank for giving you the loan) and the principal (the original amount borrowed), so the size of your debt is reduced over time.

RBA. Reserve Bank of Australia.

Rentvesting. An investing strategy whereby you live in a property that you are renting while renting out a property that you own.

Service-level agreement. An agreement that defines particular aspects of the service a lender provides, such as the amount of time they will take to assess your loan application.

Strata scheme. A system of multiple ownership of a building or collection of buildings. Property owners have individual ownership of part of the property (for example, an apartment) and shared ownership of the 'common property' (for example, foyers).

Tenants in common. A form of ownership in which multiple people own unequal (but specified) shares of a property.

Trust. An ownership entity that individuals can buy a share in, and this entity then secures finance and purchases property.

Vacancy rate. The percentage of properties in an area that are likely to be vacant at any given time.

Yield. The price of a property divided by the rental income it generates. For example, if you paid $500,000 for a property and receive $25,000 in rent per annum, your gross yield would be 5 per cent.

Zoning. The regulations that dictate what types of property can be built on a piece of land.

Useful Websites

General resources

Google Alerts: google.com.au/alerts

Company reviews and credit checks

Equifax: equifax.com.au

Trustpilot: au.trustpilot.com

Demographic data

.id: home.id.com.au

Australian Bureau of Statistics (ABS): abs.gov.au/census/ or abs.gov
.au/census/find-census-data/quickstats/2021/AUS.

Suburb data

Cordell Connect: cordellconnect.com.au

Domain: domain.com.au

DSR: dsrdata.com.au

Microburbs: microburbs.com.au

Realestate.com.au: realestate.com.au

SQM Research: sqmresearch.com.au/index_property.php

SuburbTrends: suburbtrends.com

Walk Score: walkscore.com

Government planning portals

ACT: planning.act.gov.au

NSW: pp.planningportal.nsw.gov.au

NT: nt.gov.au/property/land-planning-and-development

Qld: planning.statedevelopment.qld.gov.au

SA: plan.sa.gov.au

Tas.: www.planning.tas.gov.au

Vic.: planning.vic.gov.au

WA: dplh.wa.gov.au

Property market insights (email subscriptions)

CoreLogic's Monthly Housing Chart Pack: corelogic.com.au/news-research/reports/monthly-housing-chart-pack

Cushman & Wakefield: www.cushmanwakefield.com/en/australia

Domain: domain.com.au/landing/signup/

Herron Todd White's Month in Review: htw.com.au/month-in-review/

Realestate.com.au: help.realestate.com.au/hc/en-us/articles/115005323287-Save-searches-and-set-up-email-alerts

The Urban Developer: theurbandeveloper.com/newsletters

Wealthi Academy

wealthi.com.au/academy

youtube.com/@Wealthi

Sources

ANZ and CoreLogic, 'Housing Affordability Report', May 2022, news.anz.com/posts/2022/05/anz-news-corelogic-housing-affordability-report-2022.

CoreLogic, 'CoreLogic daily home value index', 10 January 2023, corelogic.com.au/our-data/corelogic-indices.

The American Society of Civil Engineers (ASCE), *2017 Infrastructure Report Card: A comprehensive assessment of America's infrastructure*, report, accessed 10 January 2013, infrastructurereportcard.org/wp-content/uploads/2016/10/2017-Infrastructure-Report-Card.pdf.

Domain, '2021 school zones report', accessed 10 January 2023, domain.com.au/research/school-zones-report/2021/.

T Lawless, *The long game… 30 years of housing values*, report, CoreLogic, 29 August 2022, corelogic.com.au/news-research/news/2022/the-long-game-30-years-of-housing-values.

G Capuano, 'Who was working from home on Census day 2021?', .id, 25 October 2022, blog.id.com.au/2022/population/australian-census/who-was-working-from-home-on-census-day-2021/.

Index

conveyancers 24, 120-122
Cordell Connect 61, 155
CoreLogic 7, 9, 28, 101, 156
covenants 103, 117, 121
COVID-19 8-12, 26, 42, 104,
  139, 140
credit unions 13, 14
Cushman & Wakefield 28, 156
customisation 130
cycling paths 45

demographics 29-31, 34, 36,
  41-42, 155
density 59-60, 65, 99, 102, 116
deposit, saving a 6-7, 19, 83-84
developers 85-90, 138-139
diversification 52-53
Domain 3, 28, 62, 74, 155, 156
DSR 60-61, 155

easements 117, 121
educational facilities 41, 53
elevation 63
emotion 12, 75, 91, 112, 128,
  130, 145-146
employment 3, 51-54
entertainment 41, 59
Equifax 89, 155
equity 11, 16-17, 19, 21, 33,
  59, 65, 93, 136-138, 140,
  141, 143
ethnicity 30-31
existing property 90-95, 137-138
exit strategy 56, 140, 144, 147

finance 6-23, 86-87, 91, 119,
  141, 147
financial planners 25
First Home Owner Grant
  (FHOG) 23
flexibility 18, 33, 104-105,
  136, 147
flipping 131
floor plan 64
Forlee, Ron 139

gentrification 31, 42, 44
goals 109-111, 147
Google Alerts 48, 155
Google Maps 72, 90
government policy 8, 23-26, 38,
  42, 46, 48-49, 53-54, 57, 61, 69,
  82, 86, 99, 135, 156
growth
– population 48-49, 53-54,
  57, 76
– price/value 3, 10, 31, 37,
  45-47, 55, 58, 59, 66, 73, 83-84,
  101, 103-105, 113, 115, 138,
  139, 141, 143-144

health care services 42, 53
height limit 116
Herron Todd White 27, 156
hospitals 42, 53
houses 103-106

.id 36, 54, 155
income

About the Author

Dom Nesci's passion for real estate began in his childhood. He started his career in property as an agent at the age of 17, purchased his first property at 22 and was the director of a real estate investment company at the age of 23. After completing his business degree, Dom travelled and lived overseas before going on to work as the National Sales Manager at Third.i, one of Australia's top development companies.

Dom is the co-founder of Wealthi, a national real estate investment company. He is a serial entrepreneur and investor, founding businesses in property, finance and construction. Over the course of his career, he has helped hundreds of clients invest in over $1 billion in commercial and residential real estate across Australia.

He is a genuine property enthusiast who loves to help people around him. You will often hear him say, 'If one eats, we all eat'. He has built a multimillion-dollar property portfolio, and this book is his way of sharing the fruits of his experience with everyone around him.

These days you'll find him walking around his beachside community, coffee in hand, with his fiancée Charlotte and son Leonardo, dreaming up his next property or business acquisition.

DON'T F*CK IT UP!

Stay in touch, ask questions and share your journey:

- ⊙ instagram.com/dom_nesci
- in linkedin.com/in/nescidomenic
- ♪ tiktok.com/@domnesci
- f facebook.com/domanesci

Meet the team, find support and buy some property!

www.domenicnesci.com.au

Be better with business books

MAJOR STREET

We hope you enjoy reading this book. We'd love you to post a review on social media or your favourite bookseller site. Please include the hashtag #majorstreetpublishing.

Major Street Publishing specialises in business, leadership, personal finance and motivational non-fiction books. If you'd like to receive regular updates about new Major Street books, email info@majorstreet.com.au and ask to be added to our mailing list.

Visit majorstreet.com.au to find out more about our books (print, audio and ebooks) and authors, read reviews and find links to our Your Next Read podcast.

We'd love you to follow us on social media.

in linkedin.com/company/major-street-publishing

f facebook.com/MajorStreetPublishing

○ instagram.com/majorstreetpublishing

▸ @MajorStreetPub